WINNING THE FUTURE THROUGH EDUCATION

ONE STEP AT A TIME

Praise for Winning the Future

Having been a higher education administrator for more than forty years managing programs to improve the academic success of students from low-income and first generation backgrounds, I consider this book as 'must read' for students facing challenges in maximizing their gift of intellect, whether from home, friends, environment or inadequate educational preparation. This book is full of valuable lessons, motivational stories, wonderful inspirational messages, case studies and relevant examples that make it interesting and easy to read.

It clearly promotes reading, the value of books, self-education, and the importance of selecting and maintaining the right relationships and accepting good advice and guidance along one's educational journey. It not only keeps the reader's attention, but has a magnetic pull that encourages reading to the next page, paragraph and chapter. This book will be a very valuable resource to instructors, parents and, most importantly, students from the middle through high school years, as well as incoming college students, especially first generation and students from distressed socio-economic circumstances.

Dr. Jerry L. Lewis, Executive Director
Academic Achievement Program
University of Maryland, College Park, MD

WINNING THE FUTURE THROUGH EDUCATION

ONE STEP AT A TIME

SAMUEL BETANCES

New Century Forum, Inc.

Chicago, Illinois

WINNING THE FUTURE THROUGH
EDUCATION

One Step at a Time

Printed in the United States of America

New Century Forum, Inc.
5448 N. Kimball Ave.
Chicago, IL 60625-4620

ISBN - 978-1-891438-00-4
Library of Congress Catalog Number

In loving memory of

Carmen Luisa Justiniano

who gave me life and her legacy as an author

and

Mariquita Torres Souder, my mother-in-law,

who enriched me with her love and wisdom

Author's Notes and Acknowledgements

The Souder, Betances and Associates team proved to be a positive force in my efforts to complete this book. Team lead, Laura Souder, kept me focused on the project. She lifted my spirits and as my wife would lovingly remind me of the importance of the mission of my work as a writer. This project would not have been completed without her at my side. Shawn Surber, Buddy, Elsie and Brittany Souder gave me encouragement and practical advice on several fronts to keep me on track and enhance the final product. Karla Estela Rivera made valuable suggestions related to how best to reach young readers. Carlos Jiménez Flores has been relentless in challenging me to "just get 'er done!" Carmen G. Perez provided invaluable editorial assistance. Accept my heartfelt gratitude for your untiring support and dedication.

My son David deserves a great deal of credit for coaching me to write this book. "Pops, your first book has valuable advice, but **Ten Steps to the Head of the Class** simply does not have enough of you in it." He added, "People may take your advice without knowing the context of the experiences and struggles that led you to offer it." I took his words to heart and decided to share with the reader how my compelling story influenced my recommendations for success. I began by revising Ten Steps to the Head of the Class. This process led to the creation of a new work. Winning the Future builds on the basic strategies introduced in the Ten Steps volume.

Dean Papadopoulos through his constant feedback and Skyping encounters from far away Saipan, in Micronesia, encouraged me to stay the course. It was Dino who three and a half years ago on Guam during Christmas break, helped me to think out loud how the book might be organized. His reading of the chapters and detailed responses gave me hope that the book was needed and valuable. I am indebted to you, Dino.

Many provided valuable insights and perspectives on how the book might be made practical, meaningful and readable. Thanks to: Charles Aponte, Maurice Arnold, Luis "Tony" Báez, Charles Betances, Daniel R. Betances, Julian Betances, Cynthia Betances-Porter, Misti Burmeister, Thomas Lovia Brown, Pablo R. Díaz, Michael Colbert, Lucia Mayerson-David, Walter BT. Douglas, Frank Espada, Jacob Farr, Joshua Farr, Nathan Farr, Cristina Villacinda-Farr, Fernando E. Grillo, Henry Guzman, Will Guzmán, Sylvia "Michal" Henderson, Manuel Hernández, Ifeoma Kwisi, Leonard Kenebrew, Diane Kschuetz, Rogelio Landin, Joan E. Lister, Vincent Loran, Wilson Martínez, John Matney, George Mustafa, Felipe Mercado, Jr., Luis E. Ortega, Taylor Paul, Deborah Smith Parker, Skip Pettit, José Villa, Guadalupe A. Velasquez, Angela Rodriguez, Richard L. Rodriguez, Joe Rubino, Caleb Rosado, Neida Hernández –Santamaria,

Charles A. Serrano, Joseph E. Silva, Paul Brian Souder, Christian Joseph Souder, Miguel Suarez, A.L. Taboas, Heather Tarleton, Trish Tullman and William Ubiñas –Taylor.

Finally, to those who have reviewed and provided their feedback on the manuscript so that readers might have a preview of what to expect, I extend my sincere appreciation.

Table of Contents

Foreword

This book represents the distillation of knowledge and the wisdom accumulated over decades of personal struggle, survival, single-minded persistence and ultimate success of one of America's leading advocates for minority student educational advancement. Easy to read and follow, the book recommends specific strategies and tactics to correct old (bad) habits and acquire new (good) ones, which makes it especially useful for both students and their teachers/mentors to engage in a common dialogue.

Drawing on his life experiences growing up in the Bronx, in Chicago, and in rural Puerto Rico, and on his long and successful career as a university professor, scholar, motivational speaker and consultant to school districts, government agencies and major corporations, Dr. Betances offers a unique perspective to students, parents and education professionals working to enhance minority student success. Artfully, he weaves autobiographical statements together with the voices of students he has taught and mentored and of colleagues who share his commitment to promoting student success. His perspective is informed by the writings of reading and study skills experts, psychologists, philosophers, political leaders, social activists, organizational experts and gurus on the topics of efficiency and excellence.

Where else would you find such an eclectic array of references and direct quotes from former slave, Frederick Douglass; Helen Keller; psychologist, Viktor Frankl; Mohandas Gandhi;

John F. Kennedy; poet, Maya Angelou; Lady Bird Johnson; economist, Barbara Ehrenreich; computer genius, Steve Jobs; baseball great, Dave Winfield; and golf legend, Tiger Woods?

Dr. Betances' deep understanding of the challenges faced by students whose parents have precious little educational and social capital to pass on to their children, who often are the first ones in their families to graduate from high school and attend college, enables him to propose concrete strategies that have produced positive outcomes for hundreds of students whom he has taught and mentored over the years. The book offers cogent, practical suggestions that students, parents and teachers can follow as they engage in the difficult task of coaching students to learn how to succeed in high school and college and be well prepared for life beyond, whether in pursuit of graduate higher education or the world of work.

Ricardo R. Fernández, President
Lehman College,
The City University of New York
Bronx, NY

How to Get the Most Out of the Book

Students, please listen up. **Winning the Future through Education** is not so much a book to be read but a guide to be followed. Think of it as a road map on how to study, avoid pitfalls, secure resources, and become inspired to earn better grades and graduate. It also provides useful advice on how to team-up with peers and adult partners for making your climb to the head of the class easier. Take steps to become familiar with the book's content and advice. Decide which strategies and best practices are most useful for you to implement when targeting and transforming bad study habits into good ones.

On a long and possibly arduous trip, such as is the case in your educational journey, your roadmap has to be studied very carefully and often to ensure that you are on track and moving toward your destination. Even with cell phones and GPS technology in hand, a map is essential in view of unanticipated hazards, detours, emergencies and weather factors which may threaten your progress.

The same principle holds for leveraging this 'how-to' student guide. Do not read it then set it aside. Return to selected chapters and themes as often as necessary to find affirmation, discover additional strategies and support for your steady climb to the head of the class. This book is written as a companion guide on your journey to complete graduation requirements successfully.

The Introduction, Crossing a Bridge Called Books, provides you with the context of my personal journey from failure to success through education. I was able to excel by becoming a voracious reader. You will learn how and why I was able to do this. You will meet my guardian angel who stepped out of her comfort zone to challenge me on what I needed to do to become educable. I went from abandoning high school to dropping back in and graduating. I didn't stop there. I worked my way through college, got my B.A. then went on to earn two graduate degrees from Harvard University. My goal in sharing my story is to help you make sense of why I say the things I say and the logic of the recommendations I make in the chapters that follow.

So, read the Introduction to get to know me and to discover what forces drive my passions as an educator and author of this book. Then, examine the Table of Contents to determine which chapters focus on the specific challenges that frustrate your academic progress. While committing to reading the whole book, the order in which you study each chapter can and should be based on your most immediate needs. Each step is self-contained but all the chapters together make up the successful whole –the ladder to the head of the class. You will find, in each of the chapters, a list of strategies that are essential for building the framework for a disciplined, consistent, rigorous climb to academic excellence. Be open to supplementing what you learn with wisdom from other guides and wise counsel on the topic of how to succeed in school. Reading and discussing lessons learned from each chapter of this book in small groups will multiply learning.

Read this book with a dictionary in hand. Look up words you don't know to grow your word power!

The book has **value for all students** of every socio-economic background. Students with parents who did not graduate from high school or college may find the book even more significant.

Being the **first in your family to graduate from high school and attend college** will require that you follow this road map ever so carefully.

Parents and **mentors,** this book serves as a guide to assist you in your important work. Whether you are a **TRIO professional, school guidance counselor**, a **youth worker** in a community center or **member of a religious network** who looks out for the welfare of young people, this book will add value to your mission. **Teachers** and **tutors** need to read and heed valuable strategies for guiding learners to excel. The practical advice contained herein will resonate with your role as educators. There is no more important work for all of us than to guide young people to enter the age of knowledge eager to win the future through education.

INTRODUCTION

Crossing a Bridge Called Books

I was not supposed to make it. As a poor, semi-literate, bi-racial Puerto Rican male from a broken home, my future looked bleak. I was in danger of self-destructing through addictions of choice, dysfunctional gang activities and engaging in risky sexual behaviors devoid of responsibilities. Hustling welfare or trying to make it at the bottom rung of the illegal economy would barely sustain me, but at the expense of my dignity. There was a real possibility of becoming a troubled adult, who would, sooner or later, with a long police record, land in prison. In the mean streets of my urban barrios in the late 1950s, those awful realities ruled. The truth is they still do!

By the age of 17, I was a high school dropout with nine scars on my body. The psychological ones from a childhood of abuse and abandonment were less evident, more painful and harder to heal. As a part-time dishwasher at the Rio Rita Mexican Restaurant and a military reject, I had no place to go.

My self-esteem sagged and I was consumed with self-pity. Living in the dark, damp basement of a tenement building in a depressed part of the city sapped my desire to dream and hope for a better tomorrow. In fact, I feared not living to see my 21st birthday.

However, I did manage to excel. Change came to my life. A meaningful encounter with a caring adult led me to make reading the motivating power source that fueled my journey from failure to success. I went from miserable circumstances in the hood to graduating from high school and college, and eventually earning a Doctorate from Harvard University. Crossing a bridge called books proved to be the best strategy for my way out of poverty and into the professions.

This is my story.

After dropping out of high school, I came to believe that the only viable option for finding my fortune in life and becoming a real man was to be found in the military. Two of my brothers had enlisted and now it was my turn. In the days of my youth, having a high school diploma was not a requirement for getting into the military.

At age 18 or soon thereafter, there was a good chance of getting drafted to serve two years in the Army, but I wanted to join the United States Air Force instead.

I dreamed of becoming an Air Police Officer. The thought of standing watch, protecting a mighty B-52 aircraft on a SAC base in the front lines of the Cold War in a faraway country simply fired my imagination. While on duty on a very cold night, upon hearing unfamiliar noises, I would demand to know what danger might lurk – "HALT! Who goes there – friend or foe?" If I didn't hear the right answer, I was prepared to put my life on the line, with loaded weapon in hand and finger on the trigger. "No sir, no rotten Commie agent was about to sabotage one of our bombardiers while Airman First Class Sam Betances was on duty."

The Air Force had everything I wanted. Traveling around the world sounded exciting and women in foreign lands simply loved American men in uniform. The movies glorified such exploits. I had heard many juicy tales in my neighborhood from World War II veterans and fantasized about enjoying all these benefits. The hole in the wall out of the ghetto led heavenward into the wild blue yonder.

There was a lot riding on my decision to join and I had it all figured out. To volunteer, I only needed my mom's signature. My brother, Charlie, was already sending her monthly checks from Mountain Home Air Force Base in Idaho. She envisioned me doing the same and gave the permission I needed. So, immediately after turning seventeen, I proudly announced to the kids on my block that I was joining the United States Air Force.

'Twas the night before enlisting, the anticipation of joining the Air Force kept me awake. I finally understood why films about Christmas had scenes with kids not being able to sleep the night before. My Uncle Sam was about to come through with the greatest gift of all time. A new future with new beginnings and a whole new identity was about to be mine. I counted backwards from 100. It didn't work. I tossed and turned. I told myself, "Go to sleep." It was the longest night ever of my young life…

Early the next morning, with my mom's notarized permission in hand; I got on the Roosevelt Road CTA Bus. My heart was pounding as I paid the 25-cent fare and headed east toward Lake Michigan and downtown Chicago.

I got off on the last stop and walked several blocks north to my destination. By eight in the morning, the military processing center by Van Buren and State Street was very busy. A microcosm of youthful America of every color, class and religious belief was in that building. The draft made people of every background conscious of the military and national defense. In spite of the racial tensions, the processing experience provided, at least for a few hours, a sense of unity across identity lines.

The 1958 recession pushed more men toward military jobs, whether in active duty, the Guard or Reserve. This group included recent college graduates who had received deferments as well as people who already served Uncle Sam, had second thoughts and decided to re-enlist. Scared young men of color, like me, who joined to escape being swallowed up in urban jungles were accompanied by frightened white youth running from boring and meaningless rural pockets of misery.

Some young men bunched up their courage and joined in groups of two and three. There were lines everywhere. We had to strip to our shorts and walk from one station to another.

The written exam was followed by a thorough physical. Everyone received all sorts of shots and answered questions with "yes sir" and "no sir." The adventure continued, as we carried a brown envelope with our personal records and an assigned number. Signatures and stamps of a step completed on the envelope meant we could move on to the next station. And so it went for the rest of the day.

There was one last formality before being told when and where to report prior to being shipped out to a boot camp training site. I had heard that for USAF recruits that meant going to Lackland Air Force Base in San Antonio, Texas. It was both fearful and exciting to think about the last stage in the process.

I was waiting for hearty congratulations from a real uniformed officer and to be led into a room to take some sort of oath, alongside other recruits, affirming that I agreed to serve in the military without mental reservations, so help me God. After that, there would be no turning back.

But, alas, the exit interview proved to be both brief and shocking. I had failed the written exam. "You didn't get a passing score." That was it! "Move on, son… Next!"

The Air Force rejected me without fanfare or sympathy. In their zeal to process numbers, they were clueless and unaware that they were also smashing dreams. The only door out of the West Side of Chicago had been summarily and unceremoniously slammed shut in my face.

The exam was a simple test that thousands of high school graduates and dropouts had passed. I lacked the wits, logic and practical knowledge to even do that. I was stunned, embarrassed and heartbroken.

My heart sank and my head was spinning as I headed back on the bus to Kedzie and Roosevelt Road. Returning to face the people to whom I had said farewell caused a deep sense of worthlessness and humiliation in me. I hid in my dark, damp basement of emotional anguish and despair, where there was no one to hold me, to take away the pain of being rejected and tell me everything was going to be all right. What was even more depressing was I had already been replaced in my part-time dishwasher's job at the restaurant.

The only glimmer of hope lay in the fact that after four months, I would be eligible to re-take the test. I could study a book on how to pass the exam, which was something I did not know about the first time around. The experience of having taken the test would give me an advantage over being nervously distracted and unsure of how test taking worked.

While I waited to retake the test, I needed a job. My mom visited the Italian Seventh Day Adventist

Church near Taylor and California and spoke on my behalf to the Chaplain from Hinsdale Hospital. He happened to be the guest speaker for the Sabbath worship service and suggested I apply for a job there. I rode the Burlington Line train to the Highland Avenue stop by Hinsdale, walked over to the hospital and applied. I was hired.

Ironically, I had to wear a white uniform to carry out my duties. It was not the Air Force blues that I hoped for, but a uniform nevertheless. While I was not earning a great salary, and most of it went toward my traveling expenses, I still felt I was saving face from my failure. I left real early in the morning and got back when it was dark. Eventually, I was allowed to move and share living quarters with other young men at the hospital. They were from Korea and were studying nursing and x-ray technician skills. They spoke very little English and I spoke zilch Korean.

So, we did a lot of bowing and smiling and non-verbal communication when we needed something from each other. Mostly, we just stayed out of each other's way.

The adventure of my transformation had begun the day I was hired for ninety-five cents an hour and assigned to the Central Supply Department as an orderly at the San, as the Hinsdale Hospital was affectionately referred to in those days. There, I met my boss. She was a tiny lady with a long bony finger who was passionate about education, a balanced spiritual life and hard work. She was a proud American and she wore her nursing uniform, and her earned supervisory stripes, with professional elegance. Being a consummate professional with integrity, she genuinely cared about all of her employees. She was a no-nonsense leader and there was no place for slackers on her team. Her name was Mary Yamazaki. Meeting her changed my life forever.

My plans were to work at the hospital for four months and then re-take the military exam. "You are not going to join anything until you first get an education," she said. "Become a professional through education and you will not have to start as an enlisted person at the lowest rank to get ahead."

This really got my attention.

Miss Yamazaki was outraged that I had quit high school. As far as she was concerned, the road map to success in life had to include a formal education. Finishing high school was only the beginning. She got in my face to determine whether I was genuinely paying attention. She was willing to invest her words, as long as she was not wasting her breath. She soon learned I was eager and hungry for wise counsel. The more she spoke, the greater my intense respect for her insights grew.

Yes, I needed a job. But, more than that, I needed discipline and structure, as well as coaching on how to re-invent myself for success. She gave me all that and more.

She convinced me to become spiritually grounded, be passionate about reading and pursue education like a laser beam. She taught me I had more options than what I had imagined.

"You need to finish high school and graduate from college." Her long boney finger, which she customarily waved in my face, reinforced the fervor of her conviction. "But, you won't do well in school!"

Those words seared through me. They appeared to contradict everything else she had so eloquently voiced. I was numbed by her prediction. Did she seriously believe I was too dumb to make it through school? Doubts began to circle in my head. I was stunned by the double message. For the first time, I raised my voice in her presence.

"What do you mean, I won't do well in school? Is it because I'm stupid? Do I lack intelligence?"

"Sit down, son… it's not intelligence you lack."

"What do I lack?"

"Words!"

"Words? What are words anyway?"

"Words are noises that are pregnant with meaning."

Her answer stopped me cold. Something of great significance was said. She sensed my respect for the teaching moment that was about to take place.

Once again I heard, "Sit down, son..."

"Yes, Miss Yamazaki," I responded, sitting down to listen ever so carefully.

"Let's talk about words and their connection to education."

What followed was pure gold.

That initial engaging encounter led me into some of the most amazing conversations in the months that followed. Stimulating and rich in meaning, seven mighty truths were revealed to me in the process:

1. The real hole in the wall for getting out of the ghetto depended on completing my formal education, which would eventually give purpose to my existence and meaning to my life. Pursuing a career devoid of college degree-acquired competencies would be foolish. I had to strain every nerve, save every penny and target every obstacle in order to finish high school and graduate from college.

2. Crossing a bridge called books held the greatest promise for self-actualization. Every day, I had to make time for reading, thinking and preparing myself to become educable. I had to sit on my urges and not allow the many distractions in popular

culture competing for my attention to derail my quest to excel. I needed to be on a mission to excel, pushing with all my might to get to the other side.

3. Growing my vocabulary by listening and imitating the correct way to use words from educated speakers had to become a constant and urgent duty. Keeping a list in a small notebook of new words that came my way was vital. I had to practice enunciating and using the listed words correctly to enrich my formal English speaking and interrelating abilities.

4. Reading books and looking up unfamiliar words in the dictionary had to be done without exception. The process made me aware of the power of each word in logically holding together sentences and paragraphs.

    Paying attention to each word would allow me to understand holistic plots and episodes in books. Before, reading was a hassle. It was frustrating and boring. The problem had to do, in part, with my habit of reading with a limited vocabulary. I realized I had to take personal responsibility and read with a dictionary at hand; only then could I understand the meaning of the words on the page. Reading to understand had to replace reading to claim having read.

5. Reading narratives of survivors and champions on how to thrive in spite of

adversity was necessary for sharpening my critical thinking and coping skills. This process would widen my horizons while protecting me from self-pity, and lashing out at those who treated members of my group unfairly. Sharing my learning with others would make me an interesting conversationalist and increase my self-esteem. I knew I had to become an autonomous reader and a lifelong learner.

6. Reflecting on spiritual issues mattered. My body needed to be treated as a sacred temple. A balanced routine had to include engaging in productive work, feeding my intellect, eating healthy meals, exercising and worshiping. Drinking booze and smoking or otherwise polluting my body was a no-no. Doing for others who were less fortunate without expecting anything in return was a yes-yes.

7. Knocking on the door of busy, successful, caring adults and requesting counseling, coaching and mentoring was essential for my journey to excel. I had to get out of my comfort zone and seek assistance from members of other identity groups. Think about it.

You are in danger of drowning; not calling for help from lifeguards might surely lead to death. You must tap compassionate adults nearby in order to navigate safely from hurtful poverty to success in society through education. This step would not be easy, but it was necessary.

Our first conversations about words gave context to the great truths I have revealed and shared. But it was that first encounter that ushered in the tradition of listening, asking questions, learning and acting to make great things happen.

Sitting at her feet, I hung on to every utterance about the hurtful conditions of poverty that limited my ability to become educated without adding more words to my vocabulary. Let's get back to that initial discussion:

"Yes, words – you don't have enough words by which you can become educated."

"What do you mean, I don't have enough words?"

"Students from middle-class, well-to-do backgrounds show up to school with twice and three times the number of words that kids from poverty do.

That means that they are able to understand a lot more of what teachers are saying and what is written in books."

"Why is that?"

"They grow up being read to by parents and grandparents for one thing. While adults with lots of words talk, the kids listen and absorb what they hear. They automatically add new words to their vocabulary. Parents make a big encouraging fuss when their children use complex words and lovingly correct their kids when they mispronounce words. Family members welcome the younger members to participate in conversations with adults at the dinner table."

In the rolling hills of my Island childhood home, adults always said that children were to be seen, not heard… when adult visitors came to the house, children had to vacate the living room. If you dared to interrupt an adult conversation, you got smacked on the back of the head and chewed out. More would follow after the guests left.

"Perhaps in those days, the adults figured the children would work with their backs and their hands and didn't need to understand ideas, concepts and how to learn by thinking about things." She pondered.

"Little in those days could be put in writing. Maybe visitors came from long distances to talk business. They didn't have much time to reach agreements, shake hands and travel back before it got dark and dangerous. The distractions from the kids put the outcomes from the meeting in danger so the punishing message was swift, painful and direct."

"So what's different today?"

"Parents have to prepare their children to work with their minds. In the home life of educated families, children are engaged and respected. They are taught to read so they can read to learn.

They live in homes that have plenty of books with loved ones who encourage and reward reading with hugs and kisses. They constantly see their parents read and they learn to emulate this valuable practice."

She got me thinking about things I had never really thought about. Before moving to Vineland, New Jersey, and Chicago at age sixteen, we lived in New York. When we resided at 626 Prospect Avenue, Apartment 7, in the Bronx, we only had one book. The man who lived with my mom worked in a hotel in Midtown and brought home a thick paperback book about US history a guest forgot.

For the first time, I saw a political cartoon. It dealt with a former slave. After the Civil War, with the chains of servitude cut, he stood at the beginning of what appeared to be a very long and winding path leading to a destination in the very distant future called equality. On the eve of the Civil Rights Movement, in the time of segregation, I wrestled in my young mind to understand it. A slave no more, the chains were off, but he wasn't free by any stretch of the imagination.

Once, I found a small pocket sized book about space and planets on the sidewalk near Kelly Street and Avenue St. John. The book had glossy photos of the stars and colorful pictures about space.

I loved my little book. I became familiar with its content, even if I could not understand a lot of the words and concepts between the covers. Mr. Mandel, my fourth grade teacher at PS 39, was amazed when I used the word planet in a sentence. He made a big deal about me knowing the word. I felt like a hero.

These two books, one about the past and the other about the future, had inadvertently made their way into my life. For a brief moment in my childhood, they became my friends.

I do not remember anyone buying books as gifts or bringing them home from the library as resources for making sense of the world, increasing our vocabulary and helping us to excel in school.

Breakthrough! I got it. We were book poor. Reading was a hassle and I didn't like to do it because I was reading without a compass. I did not know how or what to read.

I had not understood the process of looking up words and owning them in my educational tool-kit. No one taught me that reading was important for the journey into a better future. I was not told that reading could be full of lessons and instill pride. Never in my wildest imagination had the thought crossed my mind that reading could bolster my value in society and help me deal with the rejection and racism of the day. Through reading, I could become stronger and motivated to excel.

"What children from well-to-do backgrounds get

from their upbringing; you have to get through reading!"

"What does that mean? I mean, what if you didn't have parents who could love you into learning to read and become familiar with words?"

"You have to get it another way. Sam, you simply need to become an autonomous reader. You will need to read books, lots of them... like wolves eat meat!" She was very emphatic. "Like wolves do what?"

"You heard me. Read like wolves eat meat. You must become hungry to read. You must hunt for books. You must work hard at wanting to read. Find a safe place, go to the library. Don't let anyone steal your reading time. Buy books that speak to you. Let loved ones know you prefer books as gifts. Sink your creative teeth in the experience of reading until you understand new words and critical information about how to make it in life and excel in school."

My priorities shifted after that. I read seven books that summer and two would change my life forever. The first was The Narrative of an African American Slave, by Frederick Douglass, and the other was Viktor Frankl's Man's Search for Meaning. The latter was about a Jew from Austria who had to survive and thrive while in a death camp during World War II. These books woke me up, lifted my spirits and increased my respect for the human condition.

My vocabulary expanded as what I read added to my critical thinking about what individuals could accomplish in spite of oppression, adversity and discrimination. Reading was not a panacea to life's problems. But in reading, one would have added perspectives on how to cope, acquire an education and excel. My journey across a bridge called books had begun in earnest and I was determined to become somebody. Reading was essential to that goal and I have never stopped.

Miss Yamazaki encouraged me to apply to Broadview Academy, a private Seventh Day Adventist boarding school in La Fox, Illinois. When they accepted me, I was proud and determined to take advantage of the opportunity. As I worked through school, I continued to read and learned to do public speaking. My classmate, Roland Lenhoff, recognized this talent and taught me to memorize sermons and speeches to develop my formal speaking voice. In turn, I added to his creativity of performing on stage to get his messages across. This was the first significant collaboration based on common purposes that strengthened my educational journey.

After graduating, I attended Andrews University in Michigan. As an undergraduate, I studied one year in Puerto Rico at Antillian College in Mayaguez, to sharpen my Spanish speaking skills and learn more about my cultural identity. I subsequently graduated from Columbia Union College in Takoma Park, Maryland where I majored in history and religion.

My passion for social justice, traced back to the influence of the aforementioned books by Douglass and Frankl, led to my work as the Director of the Division Street Urban Progress Center in Chicago. I took part in racial healing endeavors after the terrible citywide riots of the 1960s. I was soon recruited by The Harvard Graduate School of Education to do graduate work there. Dr. Robert Binswanger, an esteemed professor and leader in urban education, took an interest in my work and became my mentor. With a continued dedication to reading and expanding my knowledge base, I earned two graduate degrees from Harvard and pursued qualification in sociology. While working for the National Institute of Education, I accepted a position to teach sociology and ultimately became a Professor of Sociology at Northeastern Illinois University in Chicago. During this time, I was able to purchase a house and raise my family as I taught and mentored many first generation college students, along their journey through higher education and into the professions. Today, I am a diversity consultant and motivational speaker. I travel the world to help solve urgent problems, and improve the quality of life for my family and myself.

Looking back, teachers could not have done their work of educating me, if I had not done my part in becoming a product of reading. "To go from poverty to the professions, you must first cross a bridge called books," became my mantra.

The following steps reflect my philosophy of how to achieve success in life through education.

STEP 1

Excel by Completing School Tasks Early

Procrastination is, hands down, our favorite form of self-sabotage.

Alyce P. Cornyn-Selby

WHY YOU MUST GET IT RIGHT!

Your most important asset for success in school is to know how to manage time.

Don't get mugged by procrastination or depend on cramming to retrieve lost time when you prepare for exams, do essential readings or work to complete school projects. When it comes to learning, you must apply the wisdom of Master Yoda: "Do, or do not. There is no try."

You will earn higher grades when you seize the time to meet and exceed deadlines by accomplishing smaller daily tasks that eventually lead to completed projects.

This chapter is written to help protect you from procrastination and cramming. If you let them, this destructive duo will do you in.

Exposing the Destructive Duo
of Academic Failure

Procrastination is described in literature as the practice of not fully committing energy to complete a project or task until just before it is due. Its mission is to lull you into believing you can defer completing schoolwork related tasks, without bringing your social agenda to a halt. Putting things off now, leads to feeling preoccupied later with the things left undone. The shame and guilt of catching up with yesterday will destroy today's chances for sprinting forward to the head of the class.

Wayne Gretzky said, "Procrastination is one of the most common and deadliest of diseases and its toll on success and happiness is heavy." If you procrastinate, you ultimately cram, which is to hurriedly stuff lots of information for examinations and projects into the short-term part of your brain through rote memorization. The game plan is to fool the teacher into believing mastery of subject matter has been achieved through a passing test score.

After the test, the stored information is discarded as easily as a chewed-up piece of gum. Everything you learned is forgotten. Therefore, cramming sabotages your ability to remember important information you will need later as an educated professional.

To cram is to participate in fraud. If a student successfully passes a test through cramming, he or she is certified as competent in a body of knowledge but remains ignorant. Stephen Covey says that cramming your way through school will sometimes get you by, perhaps even get you good grades, "but if you don't pay the price, day in and day out, you'll never achieve true mastery of the subjects you study or develop an educated mind."

What is the price that needs to be paid day in and day out?

- First, you must become an active, engaged learner by attending class, taking notes, seeking clarification and giving informed responses in class discussions.

- Second, you must learn in concert with others, in small mission-driven groups.

- Third, you must build your knowledge base by reading and wrestling with problems. You become a critical thinker by looking at issues from diverse vantage points.

- Finally, you must always pursue excellence and true mastery of subject matter by earning grades based on your true understanding of the literature.

Since procrastination and cramming both lead to mediocrity in educational outcomes, I have decided to combine them into one definition concept: procrasti-cramming. Without taking serious steps toward continuous learning on a daily basis, you will resort to procrasti-cramming yourself out of a jam. To avoid this, always do your assigned readings on a timely basis. Enter discussions having wrestled with abstract formulas, concepts and ideas beforehand. Seek clarification in meaningful, give-and-take peer-group dialogues and debates led by educators.

Remember, even if no one else is privy to your procrasti-cramming schemes, you are marching to receive a diploma or degree obtained by hustling the system. This leads to internalizing a damaging opinion of your own self-worth.

You Must Plant in the Spring and Harvest in the Fall

Mastery of concepts develops in stages over time. When you put in the effort to understand and complete an assignment, you build a foundation of knowledge, which comes in handy when you face your next work challenge. Each assignment builds on knowledge previously acquired. The information learned through effective study habits is stored in the long-term memory part of the brain. It allows for later recollection and empowers you to become an informed, competent citizen and member of productive work teams. At school, this process prepares you to actively participate in group projects and helps you pass examinations.

Procrasti-cramming sabotages essential steps in the process of learning. Your proficiency of subject matter is derailed. When you skip classes and/or don't do reading and course preparation on time, you miss out on becoming an active learner.

Lack of connectivity with the brain causes you to lose focus and the classroom experience drags. Your body begins to slump.

The mind becomes cluttered or wanders off. At this point, you have put yourself at risk. You are now a prime candidate for class clown, disciplinary problem or member of the Losers Club. After boredom or acting out, the challenge of having to get a passing grade must still be confronted, even though you have ignored the educated path that leads to the head of the class. So, procrastinating leads to cramming. Not having studied leads you to failure or gives the impression that you have won by scamming through cramming.

Covey writes in his book, Principle-Centered Leadership, that "in nature, certain laws cannot be violated without resulting in negative consequences. Without planting in the spring, a fall harvest is impossible. A farmer cannot plow, plant and water seeds 24 hours a day, two weeks before harvest time and expect a full, rich harvest. The laws of nature simply do not operate that way."

Similarly, certain study principles have to be applied in the quest to harvest academic excellence. Attempting to shortcut the process will yield failure.

Imagine a lazy farmer who does not plant in the spring and instead resorts to buying plastic vegetables and laying them on the ground in neat rows.

Seen from a distance, the fields of produce look ripe and promising to potential buyers. But you know the artificial, plastic substitutes are ultimately going to be revealed as a great fraud, and will not feed you!

In the demanding marketplace of ideas, we need serious students who will take the time to "plant in the spring," that is explore ideas in advance and nurture them through daily care and study so they can yield a rich harvest.

There is a proverb that says: "If and When were planted, and Nothing grew."

Why Students without Social Capital Wind Up Procrasti-Cramming

Middle-class learners tend to have parents, siblings and a vast network of people who are able to assist them, even though they appear to wait until the last minute to turn in their work. Do not be fooled. These students have been taught to read, think and tap the talents of their family and friendship networks. These networks become very creative and productive in assisting them to complete their assignments on time. If you have parents who have graduated from college, it means you have 'social capital.'

This means you have access to counseling and resources that guide you to meet the standards of middle-class places of learning.

If you are not a member of such a network, you must work harder, longer and more creatively than students who do not have to wait in line at the computer lab to complete their papers.

Often their parents will assist in the research, editing and finalizing of their papers and projects. If you come from a background like mine, born into poverty and the first in my family to graduate from high school and college, you will have to depend on your wits and not be fooled by those who make getting good grades look easy. If you wait as long as they do, you will wind up procrasti-cramming and will not earn the best grades in the process.

You are competing with a vast network of people who represent generations of successful students in middle-class places of learning.

Work hard and stay focused. Use time to your advantage. Start working on your projects early and avoid the destructive duo: Procrastination and Cramming!

The Pitfall of Academic Procrastination

Sylvester found himself cramming, even though he had studied, attended classes and done his readings for his approved history research topic. His instructor liked the topic and his seriousness as a returning adult to college. I was surprised when he reached out to me for help three days before his research paper was due. He was frantic. He could not understand why he had fallen behind. Now he was cramming. He did not like the sinking feeling as he anticipated receiving a low grade. It appeared that he had coasted until the end, but he knew that was not the case. So, how had he procrastinated and why was he cramming?

In a nutshell, Sylvester had miscalculated how long it would take to compare and contrast competing opinions about a research topic before developing his own informed perspectives on the issue. Could 9/11 have been prevented? That was the topic. The paper explored the impact of President Clinton's sex scandal with Monica Lewinsky and whether he was so distracted defending himself in Congress and dealing with his wife and the media, that he did not prevent the September 11 crisis.

Sylvester had done a lot of research and his findings were solid. What he lacked was mastery of the historical context. He needed to summarize his research and write a thoughtful analysis as to whether the events of 9/11 could have been prevented.

I agreed to help because Sylvester was very close to my heart. He talked it out with me and the paper was written, proofread and handed in right on the deadline. He earned an A for the course; however, it was very stressful. The lesson from this crisis is simple: You must allow yourself plenty of time for internalizing ideas about a research topic, in order to develop your own informed perspectives. You must discuss your understanding of the competing ideas with persons who are learned on how to make meaning of what you are studying. Give yourself time to write and re-write your research paper.

Not allowing adequate time to analyze the research and complete your assignment is a pitfall and is defined as academic procrastination. All types of procrastination lead to one faulty strategy: cramming. The good news is, now that you know why procrastination is so deadly to students, you can put a stop to it so you don't have to cram.

Academic procrastination is but one type of the dysfunction. There are others. They are discussed in articles you can Google and download to learn more.

As a young student, my primary reason for procrastinating was that I lacked an extensive vocabulary and had to read longer and slower. Looking up words was necessary, but tedious. I got better by reading more. In addition, I did not feel comfortable as a member of a minority group, so I tended to study alone. In that sense, I suffered from social self-consciousness. When I learned to make friends with those who came from homes with social capital, my learning started to improve. Luckily, the mentor I described in the introduction, taught me how to budget my time.

Early on, I tended to avoid visiting certain professors and teachers because I felt intimidated by them. Sensing my insecurities, but conscious of my passion for learning, some of these teachers reached out and offered their assistance. Mr. Gerald Herdman, my history teacher at Andrews University, comes to mind. I looked up to him because he taught me how to love history.

The more I understood what I had to stop doing, the less I relied on procrastinating and cramming.

Lastly, keep in mind that if you are a procrastinator, you have a serious condition that cramming can't cure. You may need to reach out and seek help. Amy Carlson, in her article, "Beating Procrastination: Manage Your Time. Get It All Done", puts it this way:

"Procrastination is a habit – a deeply ingrained pattern of behavior. That means that you won't just break it overnight. Habits only stop being habits when you have persistently stopped practicing them, so use as many approaches as possible to maximize your chances of beating procrastination."

The section that follows is designed to assist you in your quest to break the highly ineffective habit of procrasti-cramming.

STRATEGIES FOR SUCCESS

a) Assume projects will be more time consuming than first imagined.

Remember that careful reading of the instructions may reveal important factors not readily visible by an earlier, superficial, quick read.

It is only when you become fully engaged in the task that you will be able to notice the hidden dimensions the project requires. Always assume homework projects will take four times longer to complete than you originally thought.

The complexity of the project may also require knocking on doors of learned, generous people for assistance. Their availability and time may not be readily accessible at the last minute. Knocking on the right door at the wrong time can spell disaster for the completion of your school work.

You may also need further clarification from the educator to get the instructions right. Once you get the additional information, the task might require more research, or shaping into a final format. You must never underestimate the amount of time required to complete a task in view of the input from members of your network, the search for additional resources, updating, formatting and editing to get to the final product.

b) Activate your distraction detectors.

This issue will be discussed in greater length in Step Nine. However, since the procrasti-cramming problem is all too frequently related to the challenge of becoming distracted, the issue deserves a brief mention here.

Students today have a lot more distractions invading their study and learning spaces than any previous generation. Although daydreaming and fantasizing are still factors, the impulse to initiate and respond to text messages, view HD-quality entertainment, play video games, surf the Internet and chat can consume endless hours that should be spent studying and learning. Hormonal-driven distractions also compete for your attention and tend to derail you from your goals.

As students, you must stay focused on mission excellence. You must learn to turn the technology off and turn your respectful and creative spirits on. Success is possible for the visionary, disciplined student who will not be controlled by the artificial forces of distractions created by popular culture. Find a quiet place in which to study. Do not answer calls of any type that will distract you from your educational endeavors (emergencies are an obvious exception).

Decide you will be the master of your own destiny to excel, not a pawn on the chessboard of distractions. Put your distraction detector to work.

c) Don't let your first draft be your last.

There is a difference between handing in your first draft, completed hours before the due date, and handing in your final draft completed days or weeks before the due date. The rule of thumb is to start early enough so you can benefit from the vast experiences of those who know the ropes of organizing their thoughts on paper. Don't expect people to do your work for you. Don't expect poor planning to result in superior work.

Ask for advice and technical assistance rather than a free ride by having to buy or copy work, which compromises your integrity and limits your learning potential. Don't take shortcuts by engaging in plagiarism. Start early enough so you will be able to not only meet, but exceed the expectation of your instructors and the loved ones who are investing in your academic success. There is an old saying that is relevant for all times: "Failing to plan is planning to fail." Think about this truism. Put this wisdom to work.

Do you have the positive habit of proactively calling upon wiser, more experienced persons in your life to sit, review and assist in developing an excellent plan of action for you to fulfill all of your course requirements?

In the university where I taught, students would always complain during the last week of the semester that the computer lab simply did not have enough computers!

For procrasti-crammers, this "problem" of the university not having enough computers was an ill-conceived notion. Inevitably, they would request an extension for handing in projects.

However, the early part of the semester and well into the second half, the lab had a surplus of empty seats, or the computers were used for purposes other than completing school projects.

d) Tap the talents of caring adults, but respect their schedule.

There are adults wanting to help students grow who are never tapped by students in need of assistance. Find out who they are and how to knock on their door for help. Frank C. Bucaro advises, "Don't wait for someone to take you under their wing. Find a good wing and climb up underneath it."

Remember, you may not be able to complete your tasks on time without input from mentors who are willing to cross comfort zones, if you are not willing to do the same. I never would have made it without help from the generosity of peers, teachers and supervisors. None of the immediate members of my family had the experience of being successful in school and were, therefore, unable to assist me. I found caring adults who were not related by blood or ethnicity, but by faith and philosophy. They were not only qualified, but eager to help. In turn, I helped others in my path through life.

Find caring adults who are eager to assist you. They are not just doing you a favor. Helping students like you is what gives them meaning. Don't let them down. You can also find relevant peers who are willing to improve their grades by teaching you. Assisting you reinforces their understanding of the subject matter. By allowing them to tutor you, they are able to excel. Don't let them fail. Respect their generosity by being available when they are in a position to help. Do not wait until the last minute and lose the opportunity to gain allies in your quest to be the best.

GETTING IT RIGHT CASE STUDY

For me there is nothing more important, long-term, than getting the best education you can, no matter the price.

Justice Sonia Sotomayor

It was the best of times for young Helen Keller, who was born in 1880 to a Caucasian family in Alabama with means, prestige, power and privilege. It was the worst of times for her as well. She became deaf and blind as an infant. She had no speaking voice. Trapped in the human encasement of her body, she could not communicate or interact as an equal with other human beings in her network of neighbors, friends and family. Constant frustration ruled her emotions. She not only became dissatisfied with her physical restrictions, she became furious at not being able to communicate and understand what was going on. She wrote:

"I do not remember when I first realized that I was different from other people; but I knew it before my teacher came to me. I had noticed that my mother and my friends did not use signs as I did when they wanted anything done, but talked with their mouths. Sometimes I stood between two persons who were conversing and touched their lips. I could not understand and was vexed. I moved my lips and gesticulated frantically but without result. This made me so angry at times that I kicked and screamed until I was exhausted."

Due to her parents' wealth and position, she was able to receive home schooling at age seven from a private teacher, Miss Annie Sullivan. Through her teacher, Helen learned that communication was possible, but only if she increased her vocabulary and became proficient in sign language. She wasted no time in "getting with the program." Here is how she put it in her memoir, The Story of My Life:

"I read my first connected story in May 1887, when I was seven years old, and from that day to this I have devoured everything in the shape of a printed page that has come within the reach of my hungry finger tips. As I have said, I did not study regularly during the early years of my education; nor did I read according to rule."

Perhaps the most telling line as to why she read with such passion has to do with the catching up she had to do. She came late to the world of literacy.

She learned how to read with her fingers through formal and proficient sign. There was a sense of urgency that propelled her to fast forward the process of becoming educable and to excel in school:

"At first I had only a few books on raised print – 'readers' for beginners, a collection of stories for children, a book about the earth called Our World. I think that was all; but I read them over and over, until the words were so worn and pressed I could scarcely make them out."

It is in Boston, when she visited the Perkins Institute, where her reading opportunities were really jumpstarted. She discovered the library:

"It was during my first visit to Boston that I really began to read in good earnest. I was permitted to spend a part of each day in the Institution library, and to wander from bookcase to bookcase, and take down whatever book my fingers lighted upon. And read I did…"

She became a voracious reader. Helen readily acknowledged the benefits of having her teacher share poetry and the meaning of things with her. Nonetheless, she learned the pleasure and benefit of reading for herself:

"I preferred reading myself to being read to, because I like to read again and again the things that pleased me."

She committed her non-schooling hours to building word power and universalizing her spirit. Procrastination was out of the question. She leveraged her free time to develop her reading advantage.

Helen Keller's transformational journey is an excellent example of resiliency. She did not waste time. She bounced back from experiencing extreme circumstances of physical limitations and put ownership on growing her vocabulary and mastering how to communicate with people outside of her human prison. She could not be stopped. She knew it was up to her. She took control of her time and created opportunities to get it done.

Once her teacher helped her imagine a future full of possibilities through formal education based on literacy, it was up to Helen to become happily engaged in doing the essential tough work of preparing herself for that promising future. She was equal to the task: "What many children think of with dread, as painful, plodding through grammar, hard sums and harder definitions, is today one of my most precious memories."

She had what it took to dig a foundation upon which a magnificent edifice could be built to rise and touch the sky. She enjoyed doing the grunt work, knowing that benefits would follow. Helen was as eager to learn as Miss Sullivan was to teach:

"As soon as I could spell a few words my teacher gave me a slip of cardboard on which were printed words in raised letters. I quickly learned that each printed word stood for an object, an act, or a quality. I had a frame in which I could arrange the words in little sentences; but before I ever put the frame I used to make them objects."

And so it went. She worked at it and learned from the engagement until she became literate. She learned to read.

Helen Keller wanted to go from reading to speaking after learning that a girl in Norway, Ragnhild Kaata, who was blind and deaf, learned to use her natural speaking voice! Helen saw a future full of possibilities: "Mrs. Lamson had scarcely finished telling me about the girl's success before I was on fire with eagerness. I resolved that I, too, would learn to speak."

What follows is her explanation, in selected sentences, from Chapter 13 of her autobiography, as to how she took formal lessons and used the time outside of the classroom to sharpen her saw in order to achieve her dreams. Her great motivation for learning to speak was to make her loved ones proud:

"Miss Fuller gave me eleven lessons in all. I shall never forget the surprise and delight I felt when I uttered my first connected sentence, "It is warm."

True, they were broken and stammering syllables; but they were human speech. My soul, conscious of new strength, came out of bondage, and was reaching through those broken symbols of speech to all knowledge and all faith...In the first place, I labored night and day before I could be understood even by my most intimate friends; in the second place, I needed Miss Sullivan's assistance constantly in my efforts to articulate each sound clearly and to combine all sounds in a thousand ways. Even now, she calls my attention every day to mispronounced words...I had to use the sense of touch in catching the vibrations of the throat, the movements of the mouth and the expression of the face; and often this sense was at fault..."

"In such cases I was forced to repeat the words or sentences, sometimes for hours, until I felt the proper ring in my own voice..."

"My work was practice, practice, practice. Discouragement and weariness cast me down frequently; but the next moment the thought that I should soon be at home and show my loved ones what I had accomplished, spurred me on, and I eagerly looked forward to their pleasure in my achievement... At last, the happiest of happy moments arrived. I had made my homeward journey, talking constantly to Miss Sullivan, not for the sake of talking, but determined to improve to the last minute."

She never stopped investing her time to further her educational quest and great causes, which later defined her as a superstar in history. Helen Keller learned to talk in the same way she had learned to read – staying on task to complete her mission of re-inventing herself through education.

She graduated from college, becoming the first deaf person in the world to do so. Her story is amazing. She met with every President of the US from Grover Cleveland to John F. Kennedy. She championed the equal rights of women and African-Americans.

She invested 44 years of her life in promoting the rights of deaf people. She authored 12 books. She was a founder of the American Civil Liberties Union (ACLU). She lectured throughout the world. She leveraged her time to do what was essential to make her life valuable to others.

In 2009, a bronze statue of Helen Keller was placed in the Capitol Rotunda in Washington, DC. She is worthy of emulation as a person who bounced back from her adversity and completed her tasks early in her life. She would practice, practice, practice during her 'free time' from formal instruction to grow her skills and excel in school and in life.

Helen Keller understood the dangers of procrastination and cramming. She made it her life's pursuit to avoid these insidious habits at all costs. Her story is an admirable illustration of how one can overcome seemingly insurmountable adversities through determination, consistent preparation and discipline.

CONCLUSION

Don't procrastinate. Anticipate. Listen to Sally Berger: "The secret of getting ahead is getting started."

Catapult to excellence by realizing that every minute counts. Read ahead. Collaborate with people who are focused on success. Seek a mentor. Follow the wise counsel of those who have your best interests in mind. Don't sleep in. You also need to feel uncomfortable with loafing and leaving school projects unfinished, incomplete and unexamined. Don't let your first draft be your last.

There is a saying: "The hurrier I go, the behinder I get." Rushing to catch up because you have procrastinated causes frustration and you will find that, as a result, things will fall apart. Helen Keller got it right by working hard, staying focused and completing her tasks carefully and early. Follow her lead. Put a sign in your learning zone at home: no procrasti-cramming allowed.

Procrastination and cramming are dangerous foes. Beware of these two; they are your ever-present enemies. They will keep you from completing school tasks early or on time. Their job is to derail your chances of excelling in school.

Putting things off means you may never get them done. When you welcome procrastination into your life, cramming will surely follow.

The first twin holds you in check, forcing you to fall behind. The other zaps the intellectual and creative energies needed for the tasks at hand. Why? You will be too busy playing catch-up with the school work you left unfinished yesterday to become engaged in today's growing and learning activities. Falling behind in your studies will lead to failing grades, or phony progress resulting from cramming.

STEP 2

Grow Your Word Power and Avoid Reckless Reading

Force yourself to reflect on what you read,
paragraph by paragraph.

Samuel Taylor Coleridge

WHY YOU MUST GET IT RIGHT!

Words matter for school success; the right kind of words, that is. You must increase your vocabulary with the 'proper' words that are utilized by educators for teaching in middle-class places of learning called schools. In literature, they are categorized as 'formal' and 'proficient' English words. As you pursue higher levels of education, you increase your formal English vocabulary by reading, defining and adding these words to your repertoire.

Students from low socio-economic families face a daunting task: acquiring a larger formal English vocabulary more rapidly. While I knew a lot of 'informal' English and Spanish words growing up, I lacked formal and proficient vocabulary in both languages. That's why I had to cross a bridge called books to increase the number of words that were essential for my success in school.

If you are like me, a product of a bookless environment, with parents and guardians who lacked middle-class language proficiency and a high school diploma, you too will have to play catch-up. Intelligence and merely attending classes will not be enough to stand out.

To grow your word power, you must avoid reckless reading. Don't just plow through assigned books and articles without regard for the precise meaning of the words in those texts. Reading (and re-reading) until you understand what is written, will prepare you to learn from lectures and discussions, and ultimately aid in the completion of school projects. The benefits of being fully engaged because you understand the meaning of what you read and hear cannot be overstated.

You must read more than students who come from book rich homes and are fortunate to have family members with college degrees. Those classmates are more likely to have support systems and resources at home, which reinforce what school teaches them. They have a well-developed vocabulary with reading and studying habits that resonate with school requirements.

How will you overcome the serious challenge of competing with those students throughout your educational journey?

Why Reading Matters

When asked in the spring of 2000 why reading matters, Heather Doerr, from George Mason University, said:

Reading is an art. It is more than just comprehending words on paper. It is an interactive and lively experience for the imagination and a respite for the soul. Characters and story plots come alive in the mind. An entire world can be created simply by letting the imagination digest the language. Society today speeds along so fast that it doesn't take the time to stop and soak in life. Reading lets one enjoy the world around, through personal experiences and points of view. All memories and senses are awake when reading and yet while the outside world is still, the mind and imagination run wild. Reading gives temporary reprieve from the pressures of life and creates a new identity and a new environment. It is about learning.

New ideas and opinions are introduced. Theories are proven or disproved. Reading is discovery in its most basic element.

I love her response. It means that reading to excel will not be tedious and lifeless. It will not be boring. It will resonate with your humanity. It's about traveling around the world.

Heather Doerr talks about the imagination's capacity to digest the language. Reading is a respite for the soul. You will not be punished for taking a leave of absence from activities in the popular culture. Through careful reading, you will close the word gap in the process of making your mind and imagination run wild!

Reading will keep you strong, engaged and entertained as you increase your competencies for doing well in your schoolwork. You must discover for yourself how reading can be fun, entertaining and meaningful on so many fronts.

Confucius said, "No matter how busy you may think you are, you must find time for reading, or surrender yourself to self-chosen ignorance."

The reason why many of my classmates did better than I did in school had to do with the fact that they came to school 'learning ready.' Lessons from teachers and textbooks made sense to them, but not to me, at least not at first.

My passion for wanting to become educated drove me to libraries, bookstores and quiet places for reading. I found places to read out loud. Hearing myself say the words helped me understand them better. I became a lean thinker and a purposeful student with an inner drive to be competitive in classroom discussions. Soon, reading books, understanding lectures and completing homework tasks became easier, which ultimately earned me excellent grades. I felt alive and free from ignorance.

I had to own the responsibility of becoming educable by taking deliberate steps for growing my vocabulary. You, too, must become book rich and obsessed with reading to launch yourself ever upwards to the head of the class. The most liberating thing you can do is read books that allow you to make sense of complex realities around you.

Mark Twain adds value: "The man who does not read good books has no advantage over the man who can't read."

Both educators and the textbooks they distribute use up to three times more vocabulary words than a student with low socio-economic status possesses before entering school. You are likely to fail if you do not have as many words as educators and the resources they use in their teaching/learning platforms. The solution is to practice safe reading.

Reckless reading will derail your quest to excel. This chapter will help you target that highly ineffective habit.

Pitfall of Reckless Reading

Reckless reading is like reckless driving. It is dangerous to your academic and social health. You do so at your own peril. You engage in reckless reading when you do not bother to stop and check the definitions of unfamiliar words. Continuing on prevents you from fully understanding what you are reading. This leads to intellectually crashing as you plow through perspectives you need to think through.

The comprehension of words holds the key to meaningful interactions in teaching/learning forums. Failure to grasp the proper meanings of words can compromise your ability to think clearly, causing the mind to lose focus.

You will become bored and disengaged from new ideas that can otherwise be invigorating and inspiring. A wandering mind becomes disconnected from what must be understood to excel, resulting in failing grades. A bad report card fuels the temptation to drop out, to flee from a flunking school experience to the mean streets, menial jobs or even the illegal economy. It puts your whole future at risk.

To avoid this, imagine the undefined word in a sentence is a stop sign or a red traffic light on the road you are driving. When you discover a word you do not understand, STOP. It is not safe to proceed until the light turns green. Think of the dictionary as the light post that causes the red light to turn green. The dictionary may have various definitions for one word or concept, so finding the correct definition is your green light to continue on the learning highway.

Growing Your Word Power to Excel

Teachers use words to relay information, introduce concepts and guide the process of academic growth in the lives of students. I learned early on that words are noises that are pregnant with meaning. The more words you know, the more you will be able to understand what is being taught.

Knowing the meaning of words will also allow you to follow directions for completing tasks in class and home assignments. Formal English competencies will build confidence for interacting with teachers when seeking clarification and with peers when completing joint projects. Schools, as a result, will become what Ted Seizer called "Places for Learning, Places for Joy."

Reading is the single most important activity you can do on your own in order to become a critical thinker and a competent, positive change agent. I urge you to read thoroughly and with care.

Be conscious of your responsibility to become an autonomous learner by embracing a dictionary and taking the time to stop and define hard-to-understand words and concepts. This way, you will learn from losers who became winners.

One example is Malcolm X. He was a pimp, a drug dealer and a thug. He lived a very dysfunctional life. While in prison, he found a mentor who taught him the importance of seeking knowledge. He discovered the dictionary and how to use it. He empowered himself with words and used his new knowledge for self-transformation.

Malcolm X became a leader with a powerful, eloquent voice for social justice. He explained in his autobiography, "The ability to read awoke inside of me some long dormant craving to mentally live."

Another iconic figure in the struggles for equality, Frederick Douglass, a former slave, declared, "Once you learn to read, you will be forever free."

Think about what they said and determine that you will become mentally alive and live free by becoming an autonomous reader destined to climb to the head of the class.

Therefore, read as you must drive; conscientiously and carefully. When you purchase a summary of an assigned book, watch a movie in place of it or simply depend on someone else's interpretation, you are reading recklessly. A summary of a great book or a critical interpretation of it can add value to your reading, but you must not substitute those resources for your own reading of the work.

You've heard the saying, "Never judge a book by its cover." John Eagan further elaborates, "Never judge a book by its movie."

Why? Movie creators take creative licenses, which allow them to deviate from the author's true intent. The movie is based on the script writer's interpretation of the book. People experience what they read or hear in unique ways. Each individual walks with the author in ways that resonate with their emotions and experiences.

Think of a movie as the director's visual Cliff

Notes of the book on which it is based. There is no substitute for your own original thoughts of what a book means to you. Don't be lazy. Read! Never be satisfied with simply recycling other people's thoughts. Otherwise, you will never know the value in a story, its interpretation of research or creative perspective.

Imagine allowing someone else's trip to substitute for a real journey in which the reader and author meet and interact.

Settling for a summary of a great book, instead of enjoying the challenge of reading the author's original work, can make you sound good or even brilliant. The problem is: you will feel hollow knowing you are merely recycling the thoughts of others. Your informed voice shares with others who you are and what you are passionate about.

You are capable of original thought as an educated individual. However, you must fill yourself with lots of reading knowledge so you can get to that level.

Reading carefully and building your word power by incorporating new vocabulary into your spoken repertoire is essential.

Richard Steele said, "Reading is to the mind what exercise is to the body."

You must become intellectually fit through reading. The way you have to eat the right kinds of food and get the essential exercise for living a healthy, fruitful life is the way you must view reading, even if you are a product of a home where the wrong kinds of food and drink have been part of your daily habits, and you have grown up to be obese and unbalanced. It becomes your responsibility to break with those traditions and reinvent yourself into a physically fit person.

The same principles apply for becoming an intellectually lean, critical thinker and educated professional. Reinvent yourself. Become educated by expanding your vocabulary so you can understand what you are reading. I did.

To Stop or Not to Stop the Reading Flow

There are teachers who are half right regarding the issue of stopping the flow of reading when an unfamiliar word shows up. Their advice is to continue reading without stopping; just keep on reading until the end of the paragraph. It will become clear then. This is both true and false. True, because reading the whole paragraph will lead you to a generalized, logical conclusion about the meaning of the paragraph. False, because you will not have a precise definition of words you have read, and although they make sense in one context, they may not make sense in another. I think that advice is unhelpful, especially when you don't have an extensive vocabulary. If the goal is to simply get through the text, then this strategy promotes reckless reading, even if that is not the intent.

Be aware that teachers can also choose to ignore stop signs and red lights. You must be careful of educators who teach recklessly. Instead of pausing to assist in clarifying words that may be confusing to some students, educators will sometimes ignore the request for clarification and continue reading or lecturing. In their minds, they have good and bad reasons for this type of educational malpractice.

First, teachers are often driven by the need to complete portions of the curriculum and do not want to be deterred from that goal. Second, some teachers simply do not want to be bothered by students, who, in their opinion, are supposed to know the words and are now interfering with the flow of the course. Third, they may not care for students they have written off as expendable.

One English teacher cautions Japanese students, "Always remember that an English word may have several meanings and try to decide for yourself which one of these fits best into the context of the sentence and paragraph you are reading."

Good advice! If a word doesn't make sense – look it up! Stop and learn what it means. Then proceed.

Listen to advice, but practice safe reading. Just because people in positions of authority take shortcuts does not mean you have to. Even well intentioned, caring educators do not always know how to engage students from poverty to become autonomous readers.

Don't surrender the responsibility of developing your mind to someone else who is living his or her own reality. It's your responsibility to practice careful, deliberate and consistent reading. The dictionary must become your best friend on the journey to grow your word power by looking up and owning new words.

Why Reading Comes Naturally to Some and Not to Others

Students from well-to-do backgrounds learn the importance of reading and building their vocabulary at home. Reading is as natural to some young people as breathing. Through this process, the students build a large vocabulary that educators will use to further develop them into outstanding students. The parents, teachers and students work in unison with each other. They may not even be conscious of each other's contribution. The constant reinforcement is largely a hidden process; it happens automatically. The family and friendship networks promote reading and the learning of words and their meanings in fun, spirited ways. The vocabulary of these fortunate children grows. The benefits and values of those informal actions pay big dividends in school.

One researcher, Dr. G. Reid Lyons, from the Center for Development and Learning, focuses on why some students have problems reading and others do not. He testified before the Committee on Education and the Workforce, US House of Representatives (July 10, 1997):

Good readers are phonemically aware, understand the alphabetic principle, apply these skills in a rapid and fluent manner, possess strong vocabularies and syntactical and grammatical skills, and relate reading to their own experiences. Difficulties in any of these areas can impede reading development. Further, learning to read begins far before children enter formal schooling. Children who have stimulating literacy experiences from birth onward have an edge in vocabulary development, understanding the goals of reading, and developing an awareness of print and literacy concepts.

Conversely, the children who are most at risk for reading-failure enter kindergarten and the elementary grades without these early experiences. Frequently, many poor readers have not consistently engaged in the language play that develops an awareness of sound structure and language patterns.

They have limited exposure to bedtime and lap time reading. In short, children growing up in poverty, those with limited proficiency in English, those from homes where the parents' reading levels and practices are low, and those with speech, language, and hearing handicaps are at increased risk of reading failure.

An example I will share involves my two grandchildren, Maya and Jacob. When they slept over as younger kids, they would remind me around 8 p.m. that it was their bedtime. Their parents taught them there were certain rituals related to ending a day. Their bedtime routine consisted of showering, brushing their teeth and reading a story right before going to bed.

So they each selected a book from our children's library collection. The stories I read became both an entertaining and learning experience for them; admittedly, I read dramatically and made it fun. My wife would even scold me for making the bedtime stories too exciting right before they had to sleep. My grandson and I grew to refer to each other as 'Reading Pals.' Reading from the Captain Underpants series was an enlightening experience for both of us.

It not only strengthened our bond, but also increased his vocabulary.

My grandchildren always enjoyed being read to by an adult when they were little. Now that they're older, both enjoy reading on their own. Maya is a voracious, consistent reader. During our visits to museums and other fun places, we always make time to visit the bookstore and select books for future reading adventures.

I don't think it has ever dawned on them that

through reading, they are increasing their vocabulary, expanding their world view and building their proficiency in middle-class learning skills.

Once I heard Jacob watching SpongeBob SquarePants on TV, exclaim with loud and joyful glee, "That's hilarious!" He was using one of the words he had just learned from his mom. She used it over and over again. Then it became his.

I thought, "That is so cool." He makes me proud.

Some of us, for various reasons, did not get our fair diet of words in our formative years or from previous educational experiences.

Our parents did not have the words in their vocabularies to pass on to us in family interactions. We did not read books with our loved ones as a bedtime tradition. We did not become acquainted with the library or reading rooms in bookstores as a way of growing our brainpower.

On the contrary, some of us grew up in an atmosphere where the noises from television and the music from radio and consoles constantly blared. The noise in our homes never stopped. It seems that popular culture values everything else but sitting in a quiet room and reading.

Today, there are lots of distractions due to the advances in technology. Be aware of high tech distractions, like plugging your ears with music, spending time with social networking, or talking and texting on cell phones. To excel, you must be in conflict with the popular culture agenda and you must read ever so carefully to become educable and educated.

Remember the saying, "A reader today a leader tomorrow." Be a role model for future generations. Be there for the little ones who will follow in your footsteps to the head of the class. They will depend on you for guidance.

There is a wonderful insight by Emilie Buchwald about how reading is taught across generations in the families of educated people: "Children are made readers on the laps of their parents."

This is not so in the lives of students from poor backgrounds. If you are like me, you are going to have to decide to go from poverty to the professions by crossing a bridge called books. Read carefully to excel. Break the tradition of not completing a degree program. Make up for what your loved ones could not accomplish.

Amazingly, some of us advanced to higher grades in school despite our lack of words and poor reading habits. We went from one grade to the next through social promotions – because of our age, or because the teachers liked us, or because of political pressures on schools to move us through the system. In some cases, the teachers wanted us out of their classrooms. They simply shoved their problems to a higher level. Students were promoted to the next grade for the reasons above and not because they excelled with good grades.

For example, when I was in the fourth grade, I was very helpful to Mr. Mandel at PS 39 in the Bronx.

I volunteered to translate his lectures from English to Spanish. To show his appreciation, my teacher recommended I be promoted to the sixth grade instead of the fifth. That was it! I was rewarded for my helpful attitude. To this day, I do not know what I missed in my development as a result of my generous teacher. I do know I did not belong in the sixth grade.

Whatever the reasons, some of us simply did not make the connection between having to read and academic progress, or we did not listen to and heed the advice of those educators who tried to get us to do our part. My mentor got in my face and challenged me to read. To those of you who are first generation high school and college students, build a strong vocabulary and never stop reading.

Read as a precursor to educational success. Read for survival. Read to excel. Read as though your life depends on it, because it does!

Without diplomas and degrees, you may be tempted to cut corners and become deviant in order to take what does not belong to you.

Fortune Magazine put it this way: "Some people will lie, cheat, steal and backstab to get ahead...

and to think, all they have to do is READ." Or, to modify it a bit: all you may have to do is to learn how to READ daily and consistently, and never recklessly.

STRATEGIES FOR SUCCESS

To read is to fly: it is to soar to a point of vantage which gives a view over wide terrains of history, human variety, ideas, shared experience and the fruits of many inquiries.

Alberto Manguel

a) Learn to bounce back from adversity and increase your heritage IQ.

Select books that will make you love reading! Have fun reading books about people who were not supposed to make it. In spite of adversity, they bounced back. Against all odds, they triumphed in life. Learn their secrets to success.

Walk with the authors who have a lot to say about rejecting rejection. Find courage for your journey in hostile environments by emulating people who had it worse than you.

In view of what you have read, ask yourself what you will have to stop doing, what you will start doing and what you will continue to do in order to climb to the head of the class. Write down your answers to these questions and file them in a place where you can review them. Share your learning with others.

Read books on the lives of people who are part of your affinity group. Check out the books about heroes and 'sheroes' that share your cultural heritage and immerse yourself in their struggles by reading the most celebrated classics available. Visit the websites that promote the interests of your identity. Download a reading list from Internet sources about your ethnic, gender or socio-religious identity group.

My point is that you will be fully engaged in readings that provide useful information about your roots. Search your roots, love your heritage and continue to grow a healthy sense of self.

b) Read books celebrating famous members of the profession you want to join.

Famous public speakers and especially preachers captured the reading fancy of my youth. I wanted to become an evangelist. It was not meant to be, but I did learn a lot about the outstanding orators of religious discourse. I read and read those books until I became a subject-matter expert on the lives and times of outstanding preachers from different religious traditions and denominations. Bishop Fulton J. Sheen, Billy Graham and Peter Marshall fascinated me. E. E. Cleveland was my cultural hero as well. My dictionary was always before me during this journey.

Read the reflections, points of view and counsel of those whom you admire enough to want to follow in their footsteps. Walk with the giants of your profession and understand what made them great. In the process, you will create instant credibility with those from whom you seek letters of recommendation, coaching and mentoring who are members of that profession.

The hours spent reading in your field of interest will pay handsome dividends. When you have to do interviews with gatekeepers to professional opportunities, you can wow them. You can give concrete examples from the memoirs and biographies of luminaries in your field. You can talk with authority about the tenacity and original contributions of great professionals in whose steps you want to follow.

You can also impress the members of your family and friendship networks. It is fun to discuss with family and friends something you saw on the History Channel, a biography you have read or a documentary you have watched about a famous person you admire. You become a very interesting person to be around. Younger people in your network begin to look up to you. After all, you are educated, articulate and informed.

c) **Read for survival in school and enrichment in life.**

Students from well-to-do backgrounds and parents with college degrees read for enrichment. Laura Bush, former First Lady, and a librarian, said, "Reading will give you lasting pleasure." It will give you that and more.

However, if you are like me when I was in high school and college, you have to read for survival before you can read for pleasure. Parents without diplomas or degrees may be clueless, no matter how much they love you, about how to prepare you for the intellectual rigors of academic life in competitive middle-class places of learning. Don't be angry with them for not being able to give you what they do not have.

There are many children with parents who are not good at sports and yet they themselves become excellent athletes. They hang around people who are. They watch sports on TV. They practice until they become competent in their sport of choice. These same principles apply to reading.

Get better at reading through reading more. The National Reading Panel put it this way: "There is ample evidence that one of the major differences between poor and good readers is the difference in the quantity of total time they spend reading."

Become conscious of athletes who become TV commentators. They are the ones who played the game, but who also excelled in school.

d) Take steps to define and incorporate new words into your vocabulary.

The easiest way to become acquainted with an unfamiliar word or concept is to ask the closest person who knows. You will hear it, but you may not internalize it. You risk putting the word into the short-term memory part of your brain. The best way is to highlight the word and look it up. You can go to a traditional print dictionary.

With the high-tech resources of our day, you can Google it or use any other search engine to look it up on the Internet. The Internet will give you several options. You can compare and contrast the definitions. You may want to print a copy of the definition. Later, you can make a folder for new words in your computer. Putting new words by the mirror while you prepare yourself to go to school in the mornings is another way of remembering them.

The process for growing your vocabulary is to use new words you've learned in a sentence as soon as possible. If you do not use them, you lose them! Incorporate them into a sentence. Check out the pronunciations as well. What you will notice, as you incorporate the words into your vocabulary, is how you become conscious of their usages in your readings. Words have a way of hiding in plain sight. Use them and you will be conscious of how much they are part of the vocabulary of the educated class.

I am not suggesting that you use words to show off or to directly and indirectly put those without their knowledge down. What I am encouraging you to do is become responsible for growing your word power in your quest to the head of the class.

GETTING IT RIGHT CASE STUDY

You've really got to start hitting the books
because it's no joke out here.

Spike Lee

Dean Papadopoulos, now an accomplished
educator who recently earned his PhD, shares his
experience:

My story begins in the suburbs of Chicago. My
mother and father emigrated from a Southeastern
European country after scars and the destruction
of World War II left them spinning, hopeless and
broke in both spirit and pocketbook. When they
came to the United States, they settled in the
suburbs, rebuilt their lives and began to raise a
family. Their greatest hope for me, their little boy,
was to graduate from college.

Learn to work with your mind instead of your
hands were the words my father spoke to me
often. They trusted the schools would provide me
with the vocabulary and study habits essential to
my academic success. They were unaware,
understandably, that this foundation is only
strengthened if it is also practiced in the home.
My parents could not give me what they did not
have.

As naturalized citizens, we primarily spoke in our
native tongue. In fact, on the first day of
kindergarten, I wondered why the teachers didn't

speak Greek! I was already behind. It would take me many years to catch up.

Although my basic vocabulary and social skills were improving, I was still not reading at the same level as my classmates. I was quiet during discussions and only read the portions of the text that were in bold, as those were the parts of the chapter we were most likely to be tested on. While these reckless tactics got me all the way through high school, the same could not be said for college. My parents' sky-high hopes were crushed as my academic failure became apparent. When my first three semesters at an expensive university came to a close, I was sent a letter stating I would not be welcome to re-enroll due to my poor academic performance.

Their hard-saved money was gone and I had nothing to show for it. They concluded that I didn't have what it takes to graduate from college.

When your parents quit on you, the world stops. My world stopped. I was alone and isolated. I was failing and I knew it. So who and what intervened in my life? How did I get it right? Or, rather, how did right get me?

I started a friendship with a man who cared about all of his students, especially those who had a fire in their belly and were hungry to matter – one of his many sayings. Our stories were similar. He, too, was a first-generation college student that came from parents that could not give him what they didn't have. He was a living example with ready advice on how to accomplish my goal of graduating from college. I was ready and eager for wisdom and guidance.

The friendship that started with this wise mentor flourished. The solutions offered to me were from his life lessons and from books. "Books will show you that you are not alone. They will connect you to humanity, which goes beyond your experiences with the people in your immediate environment," he said. He was also very clear that I was not to engage in the reckless reading practices of the past. If I didn't understand a word, I had to look it up. The shortcuts that I took in elementary and high school and even in early college could not continue. The message was loud and clear.

As an adopted child and adult I felt unwanted, abandoned and disposable for a very long time. My mentor's response: "Here's The Adoption Triangle. Read it. Tell me what your thoughts about it are and what you learned." As a young adult, I spent most of my waking hours in an urban setting of one of the nation's largest cities. I wondered about its complexity and diversity and needed inspiration to navigate through it. My mentor told me to read Down These Mean Streets by Piri Thomas. The more books I read, the more connected I felt.

I carefully read every book this wise man suggested and my life changed! "You're playing catch-up for the years in high school that you spent doing everything but reading," he would say. Slowly, my failures were overshadowed by my successes. Over time, books had answered every question and problem I wondered about.

Biographies inspired me and helped me look at the world from multiple perspectives. In relationship to this, my mentor would say, "People's life stories will minimize the way you view your own suffering, placing it and you in perspective in relationship to other people's trials and triumphs." It was true. I took my mentor's advice to heart and learned many lessons walking alongside the many people whose stories I read about. I was determined more than ever to finish college.

I wanted to make my mentor, my parents and myself proud.

When I went back to school, I said a prayer, "God, if you allow me to finish college, I will spend my time giving what has been given to me." Not only did I go on to finish college, I also became a teacher. I went on to graduate school, earning a Master's degree and Doctorate, with a transcript that reflected nothing but straight A's. Presently, I teach at the college level in the only community college in the Northern Mariana Islands in the Western Pacific, writing regularly for the region's educational research magazine based in Hawaii. I am also an approved College Board Reader for the nation's high school Advanced Placement English Composition Test.

I am what I am and do what I do because a

generous and wise mentor stopped to care. He pointed me toward the power and the victory of reading books, and reading them right. Reading is a powerful search engine providing answers and solutions to humanity's questions and problems for over 2,000 years. I went from reading recklessly or sometimes not reading at all, to giving books credit for saving my life. Getting it right is alright!

CONCLUSION

Read consistently, carefully and comprehensibly. Don't rush through words, paragraphs and pages. Be a reader who wrestles with ideas, concepts and conclusions. Develop a reputation for being a thoughtful, reflective, informed student. Walk with authors who dared to dream, pushed obstacles aside and achieved greatness. You must cross the bridge called books on your way to becoming an educated professional.

Team up with a caring adult or two who will give you timely feedback on your reading strategies. Remember the words of wisdom shared by Dean Papadopoulos.

He finally launched a successful career by putting a stop to reckless reading. What his immigrant mom and dad could not give him, he got from books! You can do it, too.

If you are the first in your family destined to

complete high school and graduate from college, you must read for survival first and then for enrichment. Don't stop reading – it's essential for leading. For the sake of the next generation of children who will depend on you, avoid reckless reading. Develop a love for reading. Become a competent guide on reading and what is worth reading.

Listen to Katherine Patterson: "It is not enough to simply teach children to read; we have to give them something worth reading. Something that will stretch their imaginations – something that will help them make sense of their own lives and encourage them to reach out toward people whose lives are quite different from their own."

Recognizing the importance of reading is a crucial first step in your journey to grow your word power and excel in life.

STEP 3

Earn a Good B Rather Than a Flawed A

If you get a B while everyone else got an A because they were cheating, that's a good B to have.

Don McCabe

WHY YOU MUST GET IT RIGHT!

It's an old trick. It's easy to do and a lot of students get away with it. Best of all, it works. Well, sort of. It's called fishing for answers. You might know the routine. A teacher assigns an essay or a section of a book to read. To test compliance, teachers ask students to identify some facts from the reading by filling in the blanks on a worksheet. This usually takes the form of "complete the sentence" exercises. Specific dates, names of people, events and/or concepts that are associated with a definition are filled in by students.

The educator's working assumption holds that students can only identify these facts if they have read and studied the assignment.

Wrong.

Some students become experts at skimming assigned readings to pick out pieces of information to fill in the blanks. This habit is called fishing for answers because they scan the sea of words in search of the prize catch that will fit neatly into the space provided. I call it cheating for answers because the assigned readings are not studied. Lessons are not learned. Educational opportunities are squandered. Ethical lines are blurred and crossed. This type of fraudulent behavior allows students to get credit for successfully completing the educational tasks and appear academically competent, when in reality, they are not.

Correct Answers through Unscrupulous Means

There is a second fishing strategy. The student simply copies the correct information from someone else. That friend or classmate may have copied it from a third person. In some cases, students copy answers from papers circulated by siblings or acquaintances who previously attended the same classes. Another source for cheating is to download other people's work from the Internet, at times for a fee. Bottom line, students end up with a series of correct answers acquired through unscrupulous means.

Some educators may be clueless about this ineffective habit and praise students for their good work, believing their teaching strategies are actually effective.

If the highly ineffective habit of fishing for answers forms part of the way you do business as a student, you may want to reconsider your behavior. Although this practice gives the illusion of providing many benefits, the immediate payoffs have to be weighed against the drawbacks. Cheating in school leads to cheating in other areas of life.

Let us look at the short-term benefits of cheating for answers. The best one is that you get excellent grades – this is a real big attraction. As a skilled scanner, you can also feel good when you share answers with people who then become indebted to you. Improved test results bode well for your teacher and your parents are happy to receive good evaluations of your schoolwork.

The time saved by fishing for answers in the book or copying from someone else can also make time for doing what you want to do. All in all, it seems everyone wins!

To the uneducated mind, the least painful route often appears to be the most desirable one to take. When confronted with the challenge of reading a whole chapter, working on a complicated problem or researching a topic for writing a term paper; the lazy student would rather take the moral shortcut of fishing for answers or borrowing from the work of other students.

But does cheating for answers really prepare students to develop the competencies that are needed to thrive and excel as educated professionals?

Fishing in the Supermarket

The fishing metaphor is instructive in helping us understand why this habit is ineffective. Fishing for answers as a way of demonstrating academic competency is like announcing to your family that you are going fishing to help with the meal, but instead go to a video arcade, hang out at the mall or go to a movie with friends.

Afterwards, you visit the supermarket, buy a fish and return home claiming the trip was successful. You show off your big, fat, store-bought fish as evidence.

Your family is none the wiser and everyone enjoys the meal your 'fishing trip' made possible. You lied and got away with it. However, you still had to pay for the fish. The meal came out of some form of sacrifice on your part. You still had to work for it. You purchased a product that helped meet an obligation without acquiring any new competencies or experience 'catching the fish.' If anyone asked how you caught it, you would have to elaborate on the lie or admit not knowing.

However, catching a fish and understanding schoolwork are fundamentally different. While buying fish in the supermarket still contributes to the family meal, the consequences for the student fishing for answers have dramatically different negative results. When you purchase somebody else's research, you do not pay for knowledge that will make you sharper, more informed or competent. You are given a grade you did not earn. You are a fraud.

You endanger any mission that evaluates your academic record and concludes you have earned the right to hold a position of leadership based on your fraudulent certification of achievement.

Why the Best Students Cheat

One would think students without academic integrity are those who are just getting by and want to get through without much effort. Not so.

Research indicates that students who want to enter top colleges and universities also cheat. They use high-tech means by which to fish for answers. In the article, "Cheating is a Personal Foul" by the Educational Testing Service (1998), the following factors were documented as the reasons for the best students cheating:

College-bound students are expected to be all they can be to get into a selective college. They need to get the best grades, play the best sports, perform community services, etc. The pressure can be overwhelming – leading many students to cheat or plagiarize.

Some colleges have discussions on the topic of character and the types of people students want to be.

This brief chapter is part of that effort. You have to distance yourself from the idea that because other students do it, it would be foolish for you not to. Be strong, honest and committed to academic excellence.

In the absence of successful, effective, preventive strategies on the part of educators, you must resist fishing for answers. Supercharge your grades through hard work. As a young and honest spirit in search of true education, you must turn your back on superficiality.

Some cheaters know exactly what they are doing and are willing to pay the price of betraying their values. The Paley Voice (January 11, 2012) gave voice to a corrupt high school student in California who believed that the end justified the means:

Cheating goes against every code, rule and set of morals I pretend to follow. It goes against everything I have learned and everything I have been told. I have been told that cheaters never prosper more times than I can count, but when it comes down to it, I got an A- on the last test I cheated on and I think that means I won.

Cheating equals lying. Reject illusions, avoid guesswork, invest in yourself and take the next step. The wise student will respect a process that may take greater effort, but will yield both correct answers and an in-depth understanding of what is assigned to be read.

The Cheating Nurse and the Honest Student

"My sister-in-law admitted that she cheated her way through several exams and written papers. She falsely graduated valedictorian with her Licensed Vocational Nurse (LVN) Certification and then proceeded to cheat her way through her Registered Nurse (RN) Certification. She now works at… and I pray that her patients stay safe." Writes one horrified witness of a family member who cheated her way through school, he was commenting on an online article by Brian Bethel entitled, "No Easy Answers for Cheats; Colleges Monitor High-tech Temptations" (October, 5, 2008).

If you were ill or a loved one needed medical attention, would you want to depend on the documented talents of the fraudulent healthcare provider exposed by her brother-in-law? Neither would I.

On the other side of the moral spectrum, described in the article by Bethel in the Reportersnews.com, is Brittany Wallace, age 22. She knows the personal rewards for maintaining academic honesty are inherently sound. What is truly fascinating about her statement is her bold celebration of the spiritual victory of having maintained academic integrity on her road to the head of the class. "Grades are very important to me. I was the first in my family to go to college and graduate this past May, so that's a huge deal. There was definitely a lot of pressure there, but in a good way. I worked hard for my grades. In May when I graduated, I wanted to know – and have that satisfaction – that I have earned what I got."

Wow! How wonderful she sounds. She is absolutely sure of who she is and what she stands for. Therefore, she will not compromise her integrity. That's my kind of student. Brittany's record documents excellence. Your passion for excellence should emulate her reasoning and quest. These two examples, the cheating nurse and the honest student, speak eloquently on the price and perils of academic dishonesty. First, when you cheat, you put those who have the right to depend on your officially-acquired competencies at risk.

Second, you will never have the satisfaction of knowing you have earned what you got!

Baseball great Dave Winfield put it well when he said, "I never had to cheat; I get them with what I got."

What will you get them with?

Using High Tech Resources
to Checkmate Cheating

Students inclined to cheat have it easier these days with modern technology. The cell phone, for example, can be used as a legit research tool, or for cheating.

Explains one observer in the article cited below: "Having a browser in a cell phone puts a dictionary, thesaurus and an encyclopedia in the hands of every student."

The computer can also be used to seek valuable research information. Or, students misuse it to purchase research papers from cheat sites. They can share homework answers via text messaging and email. Some students can text classmates while taking a test without looking at their phones.

In classes where laptops are allowed, surfing for answers provides a sea of opportunities for cheating.

In some cases, taking pictures of test materials and sending them to other members of the class taking the same test has been documented. Students have also programmed notes in their calculators. Storing definitions in cell phones, an electronic calendar, or even using a watch to hold notes has made cheating easier. In some cases, students have hacked teacher files.

Ian Shapira notes, "Bottled water is sometimes banned at student's desks, maybe someone scrawled a formula on the inside wrapper?" He reports, "The warfare and counter-warfare between teachers and pupils over cheating is perhaps the tensest undercurrent running through school culture."

Teachers are trying very hard to discourage cheating. They are trying to match technological wits with their students. It's not easy. The students are sharp, technologically advanced and often determined to beat the system. If they also lack any respect for academic integrity, then it becomes very hard to catch and persuade them to climb to the head of the class as ethical, educated human beings.

The most prevalent type of fishing for answers is downloading information and claiming it as your own. Plagiarism is rampant. Educators have access to websites like turnitin.com, which checks research papers against a database of journals and papers. Test givers prohibit computers, cell phones and watches in test rooms.

Seating students in zigzag patterns, limiting visits to the bathroom during test times and even prohibiting water bottles are strategies used to guard against hiding messages that assist in cheating. The strategies to prevent high-tech cheating are as plentiful as the challenges that inspire them.

Too many students fish for answers and may even get away with scoring well in homework and examinations. While this habit may reap quick and easy results, the long-term buildup of shortcuts weakens the student's integrity considerably. The deception can be tragic.

Melissa Balmain cautions, "When you cheat, you don't learn. Since lessons build on each other, cheating now means you won't understand later material, either."

This ineffective habit is the bait that hooks you into becoming the sorriest fish in the sea of mediocrity.

You can also be exposed as a fraud and get kicked out of your school programs.

So beware – If you are inclined to take shortcuts, the day might come when you will not be able to tell the difference between cheating and studying. You will have corrupted your character and compromised your effectiveness as a productive force in our society.

That erosion of character can be halted when you decide to stop cheating and refuse to be just schooled and certified. Embrace being truly educated and universalized.

Be Authentic and Endure

Consider the consequences of cheating as documented in the Pediatric Advisor (2008). The advice is written for parents and what they should say to their children about cheating. It's an instructive piece for all ages:

- Cheating will ultimately lower your self-respect.

- It is not fair to the other students who do not cheat.

- If you find it easy to cheat now in school, you may find it easier to cheat in other situations in life.

- Cheating violates the teacher's trust.

- Cheating is a lie. It makes people believe that you know more than you actually know.

- You'll never know how well you could have done without cheating. It robs you of your self-confidence.

- You may feel worried about getting caught and feel guilty, embarrassed or ashamed.

- Students who get caught cheating face serious consequences. Cheating kids can get in big trouble at school and at home.

- In the end, you cheat yourself out of learning and out of giving yourself a chance to see how good you really can be.

Multiple choices, true or false, fill in the blanks — all of these belong to a family of worksheets that can be manipulated by guesswork. Students can guess and pass. They can, at the click of a high-tech button, decide to cheat and violate academic integrity. But they will not learn how to apply knowledge, formulas and theories, communicate more effectively, think more clearly and become universalized.

Say no to fishing for answers. Say yes to hard work, academic integrity, reading and studying.

Step up to the challenge of self-discipline and self-control as you make continuous progress to the head of the class.

Reflect on the wisdom of Dr. Laura Souder, who said, "Copies fade; it's the authentic things that endure."

So be real, be honest and be transparent in all you do in your quest to be the best.

The wise leader of one of the great Native American nations, White Elk, said:

> When you were born, you cried
> and the world rejoiced.
> Live your life
> so that when you die,
> the world cries and you rejoice.

From Perfect Role Model to Tabloid Villain

Tiger Woods became an iconic figure in the prestigious world of golf. He excelled to the highest possible degree. His name became a brand for the most successful companies to associate with.

Precision, accuracy and excellence defined his game and celebrated his fame. The fact that he was young, good looking and a person of color added to his attraction as a public personality.

Tiger Woods became legendary. His wealth grew, as well as his stature in popular culture. He married a beautiful woman. They became the parents of a lovely child. His very presence commanded adulation, admiration and celebration. All of it came early in his life. And then, something terrible was revealed that tarnished his reputation. Tiger Woods was exposed for living a private life that betrayed his public image. Ironically, he was targeted through the very technology he used to do things that were in conflict with his public values. Wow, what a fall!

Sportstale.com described how Woods went "from perfect role model to tabloid villain." Soon, he became the butt of jokes for comedians. Preachers used him as an illustration of how evil behavior can bring you down from the pinnacle of success.

While I take no joy in his demise and my prayers are with him and his family, this story illustrates how cheating in one area of life polluted everything else he had accomplished.

We are only human and can also destroy with our

feet what we build with our hands.

On December 2, 2009, he posted an entry on his web site: "I have let my family down and I regret those transgressions with all of my heart ... I offer my profound apology."

It won't be easy as the world watches Tiger Woods struggle to restore his reputation and regain the public's trust. He needs to keep in mind the words of Mohandas Gandhi: "One man cannot do right in one department of life whilst he is occupied in doing wrong in any other department. Life is one indivisible whole."

Learning from the mistakes of others on your journey to the head of the class, can keep you on track as you develop a reputation for excellence and character to match.

One of the great gurus of excellence in the workplace, Zig Ziglar, reminds us that, "with integrity you have nothing to fear, since you have nothing to hide. With integrity you will do the right thing, so you will have no guilt. With fear and guilt removed you are free to be and do your best."

You, too, will be defined by what you choose to do in the dark.

You can, at this moment, decide that cheating will not bring you down from your journey to excel. It's all about character. If you messed up and got exposed, please work to recover your reputation. If you have cheated and not gotten caught, make a U-turn. Repent and do it right the next time. If you are tempted to cheat but haven't yet, do stop and think about the consequences. Don't mess up to begin with.

Stop fishing for answers. Live with a good B rather than a flawed A. It's really important to earn your success.

STRATEGIES FOR SUCCESS

> Cheating is a choice… Not a mistake. Don't be fooled.
>
> Anonymous

a) Submit your best work, not your best guess.

Take copious notes in all of your classes. If needed, seek further clarification from teachers or students who are serious about success. When the instructions are clear, that's when you will shine. Don't leave the classroom until you fully understand what is due and in what format you need to deliver it.

Do not head home until you have compared notes with students who do very well in class. If schoolwork is to be done at home, alleviate any stress from family obligations and do your fair share of housework before focusing on school projects. Then, activate your distraction detectors so you can do your best academic work. Resist horsing around, playing video games or otherwise ignoring your tasks. If you enjoy the satisfaction of meeting your own highest expectations, you will have fun later as a reward for completing your school assignments ahead of schedule.

Finishing your work early will keep you from yielding to temptations, cutting corners and fishing for answers. If you have messed up in the past, you can work now to stop the vicious cycle of dishonest behavior. In time, your peers who continue to operate dishonestly will come to understand you have changed. Their opinion of you will change for the better; more importantly, your opinion as to who you are becoming will change as well.

The good you do in private will be rewarded in public. The reverse is also painfully true. Your sins will find you out. Your grades must reflect your best work, not your best guess.

b) Incorporate valuable feedback from those who want you to excel.

It's important that you get feedback from mentors on your school projects long before they are due. Share your strategies with them on how you propose to complete your projects. Tap their wisdom and positive energies. They will give you feedback and suggestions on how to improve your strategies and will be happy to know that the "wait until the last minute" virus has been quarantined.

There is no greater joy for caring adults than knowing you value their perspectives. Value the pride and admiration from loved ones who know you are honestly in pursuit of a quality education.

For example, I remember being on the road and receiving a call from my nephew at 7p.m., begging me to help him with his sociology assignment that was due by midnight that same night. Of course I wanted to help; however, my travels prevented me from giving him my full, undivided attention. Had he only asked me earlier, I would have willingly set time aside to assist him. I became so frustrated! There is no reason for that kind of procrastination. After all, I was a full-time professor of sociology for 23 years. Trust me, I know sociology. I love my nephew. I did the only thing I could do at the moment: I simply listened and offered my best advice.

My recommendation to you is this: if you plan ahead, you will get feedback in time to incorporate excellent perspectives. You will also have time to compare notes with other informed peers. Plus, you can further enhance your projects by going to recommended literature resources. You must be timely and informed, it will keep you from having to fish for answers.

c) **Team up with peers for studying, not fishing.**

Once you decide you no longer will copy from others, or serve as a source for others to copy from, you are ready to create a legitimate study circle! Let your peers know you can be their legitimate friend and partner for academic success. By the time you and other study buddies meet, make sure all members of the team have updated their notes from class lectures. Every team member should arrive having carefully studied the assigned readings. These small-group discussions will multiply learning.

Figuring out how to cheat and hustle for grades takes as much work as teaming up and getting it right in the first place.

Do you want to impress your teachers? Request a meeting between the study circle members and your teacher. Ask for study strategies to meet your teacher's best hopes. The teacher's admiration and estimation for all members of the team will soar. Don't be surprised if they use your efforts as a best practice to be emulated by others in the class.

By the way, in the world of work, employees with team competencies have a competitive advantage over those who do not have such skills. You will find there are so many rewards later for doing the right things right now; like teaming up to study and not fishing for answers.

d) **Climb to the head of the class with character and a clear conscience.**

When you fish for answers, you shortchange yourself because you are not acquiring the ability to read and do assignments critically. Failing to study, the information that will increase your brain power and expand your competencies will not exist.

This leads to an inability to connect facts and apply the meaning of your learning to the challenges you are facing in life. In the end, you will be awarded certificates of completion, diplomas and degrees that document your qualifications, but the reality is the opposite. Grades, diplomas and degrees earned fraudulently promote laziness and incompetence. A student who practices this habit will cheat everyone who depends on his or her professional training. Most of all, that student will cheat him or herself.

The axiom, "character is what you do when no one is watching," is very wise. There is a faulty belief circulating through popular culture that says, "What happens in Vegas stays in Vegas."

The idea behind this type of corrupt thinking is that you can do things away from home, in this case 'sin city,' and no one will know about it. Wrong! You will know about it. However, there is a danger that if you continue to cheat, you may start believing it is okay. The more you do it, the easier it is the next time.

That's why Katharine Hepburn cautioned, "To keep your character intact you cannot stoop to filthy acts. It makes it easier to stoop the next time."

When you betray what you know to be right, your conscience will alert you that you have done something wrong. If you continue to ignore your conscience, the alert mechanism will get fainter and fainter, and it may reach a point where you no longer hear the alert. Stay honest and embrace academic integrity on your journey to the head of the class. You will be able to serve others, earn a living and sleep peacefully at night.

GETTING IT RIGHT CASE STUDY

When you are truthful on the outside, you'll be peaceful on the inside.

Donna B. Forrest

One would be hard-pressed to believe that a teacher would enter an Adult Literacy Center needing to learn how to read. That is exactly what John Corcoran did. In his powerful memoir, The Teacher Who Couldn't Read, he takes us through his life and the events that led him to publicly say the following:

Yes, I am a graduate of a university, with a bachelor's degree in education and business administration. I have completed 90 additional graduate hours in education, economics and sociology at more than four major universities.

I attended school 35 years, half of those years I

was a professional educator. It may be incredible or shocking to some, but it is undisputable that in acquiring these experiences, I could not read a textbook or write the answer to an essay question... I have been a functional illiterate for almost 50 years.

These were the powerful words John Corcoran spoke at an Executive Breakfast hosted by the San Diego Council on Literacy and the San Diego Chamber of Commerce. What he was saying sounded unbelievable to those present. This would be the beginning of a series of testimonies he would give about how he spent his life fishing for answers as he hid his secret of illiteracy.

Corcoran came from a large Irish-Catholic family. He had hard working parents who valued faith, family and education. His mother was their rock; she enforced good manners, cooked healthy meals and stretched every dollar to take care of her many children. His father was a teacher who went anywhere there was work. Their greatest desire was for their children to be college educated.

Because of the teaching assignments Corcoran's father took, the family moved around a great deal throughout the southwest. Although Corcoran was exposed to children from various racial/ethnic backgrounds, he dealt with a lifelong sense of alienation.

With every school he attended, he found new ways to get through the year without exposing his major weakness. But instead of shying away from the challenges of school and failing, he learned his way. In grade school, he developed signaling patterns with his friends, who gave him answers to exams. He also copied assignments and made friends with the high achievers, using their discourse and smarts to gather information vital to pass his classes. Instead of reading books, he picked the brains of those who did read, keenly memorizing their words and making them his own in the next day's oral book report.

The older he got, the harder it was to turn back. In high school, he affectionately asked his girlfriend, Mildred, to read him the questions in their math homework. A consummate gentleman, he later let another girlfriend order first in a restaurant.

Then, he simply said, "I'll have the same," in order to avoid the embarrassment of not being able to read the menu. In college, his fraternity brothers assisted him in obtaining answers to major exams. For them, it was just a college prank. For him, it was his key to surviving. He did not want to let his family down by not finishing.

Corcoran indeed graduated from college and went on to teach high school, creating seating charts that allowed him to memorize his students' names and having them grade each other's work in order to perpetuate the façade.

He was always afraid that he would one day be called out on his illiteracy. As a child and teen, frustration over this secret manifested itself in school fights. He was afraid someone would blow his cover. In his adulthood, this pent-up frustration made him defensive; he often reacted with outbursts to simple situations. Only his wife knew the reason behind it and she tried to ease tense situations in public places. He could not even read a bedtime story to his children. A series of events threatening his livelihood, family and marriage led John Corcoran to a breaking point. He knew something had to be done.

In 1986, a college graduate, teacher, father and business owner walked through the doors of the Adult Literacy Center and asked for help. It was there he was challenged and inspired by the coordinator, Lynda Jones, who paired him with tutor Eleanor Condit. They pieced small words together and began reading major periodicals by sounding out and using phonetics. The process took time. Condit encouraged him to begin a journal, which he later shared with her. Together they fixed the words that were misspelled. It was empowering. He no longer felt like an alien in his own world.

John Corcoran went from being the poster child of fishing for answers to the spokesperson for nationwide literacy programs alongside former First Lady Barbara Bush. His story not only speaks to the notion that we are all capable of being lifelong learners, it also teaches us the lesson that fishing for answers for any period of time hurts a student more than it helps. While diplomas legitimized him, the secret he kept for nearly forty years permeated everything he did until he decided to make a change. Once he decided to take action to remedy the situation, his anger subsided and he was no longer living the double life of a teacher who could not read.

CONCLUSION

Fishing for answers will ultimately hurt you more than anyone else. You can choose to become a fraud, just like John Corcoran. Or, you can become a champion, like Mr. Corcoran did the day he walked into a literacy center in search of assistance. As an adult, he decided to let go of his burden by learning how to do it right.

You don't have to wait that long. If you are doing it wrong, stop and seek assistance now. If you continue to cheat you may be able to obtain diplomas, pass courses, earn credit hours, and even graduate, all the while falling short of becoming educated and competent in the ways that your grades and certificates imply.

Or, like Tiger Woods, you can lose on so many fronts when you are eventually exposed. Be mindful of the lessons from this tragic story of a young champion. Todd A. Smith in his online Regal Magazine writes, "Woods' situation is a reminder to all, not just the rich and famous, that one mistake can cause one to lose all they have worked for. And although it is quite possible that one can rebound from past mistakes, sometimes a mistake can cause people to never view you the same as they once did."

You could get caught, exposed, embarrassed or expelled from courses and learning programs. Refuse to put yourself in harm's way. Team up with serious minded peers and don't take shortcuts. Be proud of your true achievements. Be honest and enjoy the benefits and values of a true education.

STEP 4

Read Before and After the Lecture

Reading before classes lets you show that you're ready, that you care, and that you are intelligent.

Dr. Tara Kuther

WHY YOU MUST GET IT RIGHT!

Knowing how to read is vital for becoming educable. Consistent reading will increase your intelligence. Strategically doing so before and after each class lecture is very important. Pre-lecture reading qualifies you to become fully engaged in the community of scholars. Post-lecture reading reinforces what is worth knowing and remembering from class discussions, projects and tasks. Both types of reading will earn you positive evaluations on your quizzes and exams, and as an active participant in class. To excel, you also have to practice the seven steps in-between pre and post lecture reading as follows:

1. Attend every class and sit close to instructors

2. Focus on the lectures and avoid distractions

3. Participate in the exchange of ideas and take copious notes

4. Seek clarification from teachers on readings and lecture points

5. Always look up definitions for unfamiliar words and concepts

6. Routinely rewrite your notes and correct any scribbling

7. Prepare for exams and projects with peers and mentors

Some students believe they can excel without exerting themselves to do the above. Don't be one of them. Refuse to gamble that you will not be exposed by the teacher for showing up to class unprepared. You will feel vulnerable, insecure and stressed. Your preoccupation over possibly being smoked out will distract your concentration from what is being taught in the classroom.

Claim your identity as a hard-working, passionate emerging educated professional. Exert yourself by reading, following the seven steps, re-reading, acing the tests and owning and leveraging knowledge while climbing to the head of the class!

The Benefits and Value of
Pre and Post Lecture Reading

Don't expect to fully understand what is contained in your pre-lecture readings. Educators do not expect you will. That's not the reason for pre-lecture reading. P.D. Nolting, in Math Study Skills Workbook, tells why:

Instructors do not expect students to understand everything when they read ahead. However, the students who read ahead will get more out of the class because they have insight into the direction of the next day's lecture. By reading ahead the students can prepare questions for the following day's lecture. The next day the students will know what parts of the instructor's lecture require their complete attention.

If their questions are not answered within the lecture, the students are already prepared to ask the instructor. (Boston, MA: Houghton Mifflin, 2008)

You must read ahead. Show up to class ready to be engaged in the process of critical thinking and fully committed to participating in meaningful discussions that multiply learning. Re-reading assignments after discussing them in class sharpens your understanding of the material. Your ability to recall lessons learned will be enhanced.

Faulty Assumptions about
Pre- and Post-Lecture Reading

1) Assuming that reading only after the lecture is an effective way to get by.

When you do not prepare before the lecture, you will undoubtedly show up without having anticipated questions and points to be clarified. Trust me, you will miss out on how to make intellectual sense of what is being discussed and must be learned. You must strive to acquire a holistic sense of the subject matter and how things are connected. This requires preparation.

Pre-lecture reading is not pointless or double-work as some may think. It's a critical first step in developing your knowledge base and deepening your understanding of curriculum materials.

Post-lecture reading reinforces what you read earlier and helps make sense of questions you had and clarifications you and other classmates sought during class discussion. The synthesis of ideas and concepts in the learning exchange is made possible by both pre- and post- lecture reading.

2) Believing that it is not necessary to read portions of the assigned text that will not be covered in quizzes and exams.

Some educators casually announce what sections in reading assignments will not be covered in exams. This tends to happen when teachers depend on tests prepared by book publishers. You might be tempted to believe that such announcements are good news. But think again – the ignored information will create gaps of knowledge. You will likely pay the price for these gaps later in your studies. In more advanced courses, the instructors will assume that you have mastered all of the important pre-requisite materials, even if you were not tested on them.

The best students will read more than what is required in order to master the subject matter, not just ace a test. Don't accept a free ride to mediocre destinations from anyone, including cavalier educators.

Your destination is to the head of the class. To get there, you must prepare thoroughly.

3) Believing that socializing is better than pre-lecture reading; so, reading to catch up afterwards will have to do.

Self-gratification or competing 'feel good' agendas may be far more appealing than having to read before going to class. Helen Keller cautions, "True happiness … is not attained through self-gratification, but through fidelity to a worthy purpose."

Pursuing formal educational competencies is a worthy purpose. It does require focus and discipline for putting first things first. You need to defer gratification to pursue education as the main priority on your agenda. Sit on your urges.

Say no to 'feel good' distractions. Avoid thinking of post-lecture reading as your "go to the head of the class" card. It does not work that way. A post-lecture reading strategy builds on the good habits that preceded it through pre-lecture reading and classroom discussion.

4) Guessing when teachers will give exams or quizzes as your cue for doing assigned reading.

For example, after a major test has been given, you may correctly expect that the teacher will not 'spoil' the next class by giving a quiz. Students deserve to get a 'breather' after a period of rigorous preparation for a test, right?! You might also assume the teacher will be too busy grading the previous exam to add to their pile of papers in need of grading and recording. This might lead you to abandon reading assignments right after taking an exam or test. In college settings, some students may not even attend the following class!

If you are tempted to think like that, resist the impulse. Don't let your guard down. Even if you get a breather after a test, don't outsmart yourself by skipping out on the education you paid for. Study carefully, show up to class, participate and keep reading ahead. As Mr. Hallock, my science teacher, used to say, "Show up prepared – get your money's worth."

5) Assuming that reading the headings and closing paragraphs will give you the whole picture.

Not so. Shortcuts seldom work to provide the framework needed to master anything of value.

Listen to the wisdom of Beverly Sills, "There are no shortcuts to any place worth going."

If you show up barely prepared and can't answer when called upon, your teacher may quickly surmise that you can't be counted on to contribute meaningfully to class discussions. Be very careful. Educators learn to ignore the disengaged students. You will be written off as a superficial, intellectually lazy or undesirable student – a loser.

Choose to be part of the community of learners. Show up informed and eager to participate. Shortcuts will prolong your journey to the head of the class.

6) Believing that you can skip going to class altogether and still learn.

Some college students mistakenly rely on just doing the readings to get a passing grade. "Just read the textbook and take the exam" is their motto. This strategy is tantamount to committing intellectual suicide. While some instructors lean heavily on what is written in the textbook and on the tests provided by the publishing companies in their Instructors' or Teachers' Editions, they also factor in other measures in their final evaluations.

Some may give essay questions in the test that are related to what was taught from other sources in the course. The context for such questions is often based on discussions and analyses of themes and topics not included in the textbook.

Don't gamble your academic journey on the hopes that all you have to do is read to study for exams. Engage yourself in class discussions and become universalized and well-educated in the process.

7) Pretending to be a student by faking pre- and post-lecture reading and everything in between to meet academic requirements.

Impostors in the classroom depend on their wits and creativity to act like good students and get passing grades as a result of their phony participation. For them, getting by is what counts. The differences between a real student and pretenders are discussed in a lecture published in 2009 by Miles College entitled, "Classroom Deportment for the Real Student" as follows:

Therefore, the real student is a person who likes to go to class for the learning opportunities that are possible; a person who seeks knowledge and understanding; a learner who tries to relate the knowledge being acquired to other learning in other classes, to things that are happening in life, to things that are occurring in the world and to what he/she is thinking and feeling. The real student enjoys learning and studying although he/she does not always find doing so to be easy, nonetheless, he/she has learned to enjoy the challenge that studying offers.

On the other hand, pretenders:

• Think teachers MUST entertain students to prevent boredom;

• Do not really like attending classes, but think they may pass the class simply because they did attend with some frequency;

• Think that the knowledge they acquire through the course has nothing to do with real life and is only to be memorized, remembered for the teacher's quizzes and tests, and then forgotten;

• Look for excuses not to perform learning tasks, refusing to try, feeling satisfied with saying, "I've never done that; I don't like to; I don't have time, if…"Expect to be given good grades, either for trying to learn or saying they are trying, even when the results are negligible;

• Attend classes to sullenly RESIST learning or to be the class clown;

• Have the unmitigated gall to challenge, intimidate, and denounce teachers who dare to give the poor grades that negative classroom DEPORTMENT earned; and,

• Cut classes, refuse to study, will not prepare homework with top effort that results in both learning and earning a grade, yet demand an A, B, C, or D of the teacher.

There you have it – an exposé of both genuine and fake students. My advice for you is to always keep it real. Don't pretend.

Be an Active Reader not a Passive One

The purpose of education is to increase your value to humanity. Your passport to effective participation in the classroom is determined by your preparation. By not delving into the assigned readings before class, you cheat other students from a point of view that can contribute to everyone's learning. Your physical presence in class simply wastes the room's oxygen. Don't choose to remain ignorant. You should read to inform your opinion and develop your own perspectives. Then you can compare your ideas with other equally informed opinions and add value to the class.

When you read to satisfy the demands of an outside authority, you have an erroneous sense of the function and impact of reading on human understanding. Post-lecture readers are more interested in obtaining a certificate to be hung on a wall than they are in achieving the proficiency that can be applied to solving urgent problems. Avoiding course-required reading assignments is likely to lead to not wanting to read later in life. The world of work is complex and constantly changing. If you do not become an autonomous reader in your field, you will not increase your competencies for addressing professional challenges. If you become a reader today, you can become a leader tomorrow.

Be conscious of the fact that some educators will not care if you become a reader or not. Teachers will tell you what is required and expect you to do the essential work they have assigned. As far as they are concerned, their job is to grade your performance, not encourage you to excel.

I have had teachers who either did not care or were in no position to take a personal interest in my academic journey. Then there was Mr. Gerald Herdman, who encouraged me to study the right way.

Mr. Herdman was my history teacher at Andrews University. He told me to pre-read the assigned portions of the textbook twice before attending class, "Doing so will make you familiar with the text. Reading it the second time will deepen your understanding of the most important points. You will show up with lots of information. My job is to give meaning to the text. You can only appreciate the meaning if you have read the text before you come to class."

After incorporating his strategy for the semester, I took the final examination in my European history course. I will never forget when Mr. Herdman called the dorm and asked for me. It was the only telephone call I received while in college. I rushed down the hall to the phone booth and he said, "Sam you missed a B by two points." I was disappointed. Then I heard him chuckle. "The fact is, you got an A!" My grade was two points above a B. I thanked him profusely and I will never forget that he took the time to call me.

Mr. Herdman knew how much I cared about doing well in college. He also knew I had no relatives or family connections investing in my quest. So, when I asked if he would go to the Father and Son Banquet at the University with me, he agreed. We made an interesting and conspicuous pair, I am sure. Our conversations about history brought our spirits together. I would ask great questions that he loved to reflect on. He knew I valued the way he taught and I knew he valued the way I learned.

My preparation and eagerness to participate in class discussions pleased him. He felt secure in the knowledge that I was not pretending to be a student. Like Mary Yamazaki before him, he saw how fully committed I was to re-inventing myself by reading and studying. He wanted to assist me in my quest to become a competent, educated professional. I needed encouragement, coaching and mentoring and I welcomed his intervention.

It was in his class that I first became somebody. Pre-lecture reading prepared me to voice an informed opinion in class discussions. The other students seemed impressed with my passion for the subject and willingness to express my views.

I became a tutor for students from the West Indies who did not have a background in American history. Reading for tutoring prepared me to become very engaged in the courses. The more I shared with them, the more I internalized. They learned and excelled, and I learned even more. As a result, I performed exceptionally well on my exams and declared History as my major.

Having a coach and mentor in your field of study is awesome. Thank you Mr. Herdman – I owe you and I continue to pay you back with my success.

In the blog Academictips.org, Roger Solberg writes in his article about reading and highlighting tips:

One of the most frequent things I say to students is to be an active reader not a passive one. Reading isn't like watching TV. You just can't stare at a page, and expect to remember much. Read an assigned chapter quickly – first for a general overview – then go back and seek out details. Keep a pen or a pencil, not a highlighter, in your hand. Underline passages. Write notes, questions and reactions in the margins. When you read you should be having a conversation with the text. Don't let it do all the talking – react to it.

Your response helps you to formulate the meaning of the text. Mark your book like crazy. I always tell my classes; the more you decrease the value of a book- the more you're probably getting out of it. So remember, read actively.

Own the textbook! I love Professor Solberg's passion for actively engaging with the author.

Professor Solberg is my kind of teacher. Please heed his wise counsel. Claim the responsibility for learning what's inside of those books of yours. Make it your personal goal to grow intellectually.

You should attend class and learn from informed discussions; however, you should also treat your books as separate, invaluable resources that have information, concepts and lessons to teach you. In order to reap the benefits, you must actively become engaged in reading to increase your knowledge.

STRATEGIES FOR SUCCESS

Leisure reading makes students more articulate, develops higher order reasoning, and promotes critical thinking.

National Endowment for the Arts, (2007)

a) Read to enter the zone of self-directed learning.

Teachers will tell you what to read and when to read it. Follow their lead. Then, become your own guide. You must graduate from becoming an externally motivated learner to one who responds to internal signals. Remember, the goal of self-directed learning is the true aim of education. When you read to satisfy your hunger and thirst for acquiring useful knowledge, then you will truly be on the path to the head of the class.

Take charge of your own personal learning agenda. Decide to read what has been assigned because you realize the importance of following through. You can learn to control the pace, the depth and the amount of pre- and post-lecture reading you do.

Choose where you sit in class wisely. Strategically sitting where you can hear well and gain the most from the facilitator of the course is so important. When people go to a concert, movie, play or sports event, they shop for the best seats. They don't want to sit too far back or in front of obstructions. In becoming a self-directed learner, you, too, must shop for the best seats in the house. Enter the zone of self-directed learning.

b) **Multiply learning through participating in group discussions.**

Build your self-esteem by expanding your contribution to class discussions. To be recognized and celebrated by your teachers, you must engage yourself in the exchange of ideas as an informed member of the community of learners.

Pre-lecture reading qualifies you to become engaged and expand on what the book says. When you open your mouth and exude wisdom and useful knowledge, your reputation will grow. You can also take issue with conclusions by others engaged in the exchange of ideas. With supporting evidence from other sources, you can express your opinion with authority and command the respect of your peers and educators.

You need to read much more than your teachers require. Intense, mission-driven discussions are only possible when the reading part of the homework has been done. Lacking knowledge on what the textbook focuses on will keep you quiet and on the sidelines.

You want to get really close to people worth having as friends; listen to their opinions.

Feel their passion for what is really worth knowing. Take part in a true exchange of ideas with them. Love learning and being around others who love the same thing; that way, you will always have great conversations on your journey through life.

In the age of social networks, there is a temptation to believe that with a click of a button, a friendship is created. Virtual friendships can be fleeting. Don't get fooled. Those quick and superficial 'relationships' will not last. Educational platforms provide a better alternative for cultivating life-long friendships. Transform yourself into a powerful, universalized, attractive, informed and resourceful individual whom others want to pursue as a valuable colleague and friend.

c) Read once for familiarity and twice for deepening your understanding.

When reading an assignment, you may come across key concepts that must be put to memory. You may need to explain and make sense of what you are reading in class or to study buddies. That is why you should read something once to become familiar with the content and then again to deepen your understanding.

While it is hard work to read something twice, the struggle to understand important details and focus on significant conclusions is more enjoyable and enriching the second time around.

d) Earn extra credit by doing outside/recommended readings.

One of the secrets to academic success is to do 'outside' readings. Educators will recommend additional sources to compliment the textbook. Ask the teacher if you can read an extra book related to the subject for extra credit. Reading memoirs of the giants in the field you are studying can prove to be exciting and meaningful. The instructor can then provide guidelines on the type of report or exercise that will be utilized to evaluate your extra reading.

Doing extra readings helped me calm my fears as a first-generation college student who dreaded taking examinations. I would go to my teachers and request permission to do additional book reports. Some did not allow it, but most did. This process allowed me to earn extra credit. When I became a professor of sociology, I often encouraged students to read two additional books.

They would provide a report on the meaning of the books and how lessons learned applied to the challenges they were facing. If they completed everything else required plus the two book reports, then they would receive a letter grade higher in the course.

GETTING IT RIGHT CASE STUDY

> If someone does not know about the basic workings of a system, how are they going to operate within the system successfully?
>
> Annette Smith

Gladys Santiago is a consummate professional who, as a Latina growing up in the hood, did not always know how to get it right. This is her story:

For almost two years, I felt invalidated. I was placed on academic probation and required to take mandatory English and Math tutorial sessions. In the basement classroom of the Observation Tower located at the edge of campus, I would contemplate why I was wasting time on these courses. After all, I graduated from high school with a college-prep curriculum and I received good grades in Math and English. Simultaneously, I would wonder why I was not progressing as quickly as other students.

What did they have that I did not? I later learned they had attended better schools and had people in their lives well versed in navigating college. They were taught good study habits and were expected to do better than "just enough."

I had fallen behind the college course schedule by having to take remedial courses. What difference would one or two years make? It meant taking on an additional $20,000 in student loans.

On top of that, I would find myself dealing with other personal challenges that would put my becoming the first in my family to graduate from college in jeopardy. However, none of that mattered as much as my desire to secure my degree. I knew it was my ticket to freedom, allowing me to get on with my real life, earn my own money and make a difference in the world. However, I will say that many of the bumps and bruises would have been avoided had I only been better prepared.

I wish someone in high school would've explained what a core curriculum was. I wish someone taught me study habits and the importance of participating in study groups.

I wish someone was there to tell me not to settle with the school-assigned advisor and find that special person(s) who had my best interest in mind. I knew I wasn't stupid, but I was close to calling it quits, until one early morning economics class. The professor asked me to stay afterwards. He told me he was impressed with my grasp of economics and said I was a very bright student. But he then scolded me about how I was wasting my time partying and not taking college seriously. I wondered how he knew what I was doing on campus.

Unbeknownst to me, I was conditioned to be lazy. I simply did enough to get by. I learned to create and take shortcuts. I would miss first day of class, wait to buy the book, cram for exams, go party with friends and skip vital study sessions. Moreover, I didn't ask for help and invalidated tutoring. He knew this and more. And for some reason, he also knew I needed a hand-up in the world of conditioned handouts. He then spoke the words that would change my life: "I will help you." Those words put me in a trance-like state.

At our next meeting, he pulled from his desk drawer the course schedule for the next three years.

We created a plan that enabled me to achieve a double major, double minor, an independent study and a self-sought field internship, all within three years! Our plan prepared me to take the senior level courses, which only came around once a year. This was important so as to not have to wait around another year to take the course. He taught me how to prepare for class. First, he de-mystified the notion that the first day of class was unimportant. The instructor revealed a great deal about what to expect and how to ensure success. He advised me to buy and pre-read the book before the first day of class.

He stressed the importance of becoming familiar with the book by reading the entire preface and foreword, the complete first and last chapter and the first paragraph and last paragraph of each chapter. He warned that waiting until after the lecture to read would not allow me to fully understand the materials being discussed in the classroom. He further taught me how to find and form study groups and project teams that would enable me to fully engage in topics discussed during and outside of class. For my independent study, he provided guidance on researching sources relevant to the course of study.

He was my true advisor. Although I had been conditioned to be lazy, he was able to hone in on my talents and assist me in learning and applying the very basic principles of success:

- Intentional work ethics - How can it be hard work when it's for a purposeful intent?

- Stray from the status quo; make your life happen - Do you want to be like most people who are simply letting life pass them by?

- Ask for help and don't settle for the assigned people in your life - My college-assigned advisor began to view me in a different light after the third signing of my course schedule. Eventually, he, too, asked me to help on a couple real-world projects.

Graduation day finally arrived. Faculty and staff were seated on the other end of the stage. After receiving my diploma, I stopped and looked right at my professor and thanked him. He stood up and said, "Gladys, it is a student like you that makes me proud to be a professor." Rest assured -- there are many people waiting to say to you what my professor told me on graduation day.

Seek them out, ask for help and never give up on your quest to the head of the class.

Gladys' parents did not attend college and could not help her. Gladys fumbled initially, but finally figured things out and welcomed her economics professor as a mentor. She discovered the secrets to being well prepared. So can you!

CONCLUSION

Become fully engaged and competitive in your classes by being prepared. Having read, reflected and studied the concepts in class assignments, you should enjoy the exchange of ideas that will likely follow. Grow intellectually as you begin to connect the dots and understand things abstractly. Take copious notes, pay attention and be in full control of what is happening in your brain. Become an active student.

Joe Landsberger's website on Study Guides and
Strategies is a good example of the kinds of
resources available online. His advice on taking
notes from a textbook is particularly relevant to
deepening your understanding of what you read.
Consult with these and other useful how-to
guides to enhance your study skills.

Embrace the lessons that will increase your
competence as an emerging critical thinker and
professional. Be assertive and look for someone
who cares and can guide you toward success.
Don't ever attend a class lecture uninformed
about the topics to be discussed, debated and
dissected. Read before and after lectures. Your
climb to the head of the class depends on it.

STEP 5

Leverage Free Time to Sprint Ahead

The best intelligence test is what we do with our leisure.

Dr. Laurence J. Peter

WHY YOU MUST GET IT RIGHT!

Study halls, after school hours, weekends, holiday pauses, long summer breaks, traveling long distances, down time while waiting for services, teacher/staff training days and emergency school closings are too frequently used for a plethora of time wasting activities. You see people texting, talking on the phone, gossiping, snoozing, watching TV or maybe doing some light reading; however, you rarely see any self-initiated study.

Think of these times as study-bonus opportunities, not as time to kick back and relax with friends or sleep. What follows is the business case for getting rid of the highly ineffective habit of loafing during the time you should be studying.

Let us look at study hall periods (allotted class periods in many US school systems in which students do not have a formal academic subject scheduled). The 'free' study hall period can be utilized by the student as he/she chooses to advance his/her academic agenda. Since the study hall session occurs during the regular school day, students are encouraged to use the period to stay focused on academic tasks. Ideally, this is the perfect time to catch up on pending homework assignments, work on upcoming projects, read ahead and focus on quiz/test preparations. For those who know how to utilize it, study hall can prove to be a blessing in disguise.

One of the complaints many students voice is that they are always told what to do and don't have an opportunity to make their own decisions. Study hall is ideal for exercising one's own strategy for using time wisely. In theory, then, study hall is an oasis. It is an opportunity to use breaks in the regular study schedule to fulfill academic requirements at your own discretion. Students are expected to demonstrate maturity by exercising self-control and self-directed learning. All too frequently, study hall amounts to a colossal waste of time.

Through the years, students have wasted study hall time in different ways. In your parents' or even grandparent's generation, students looked through magazines, secretly passed notes and tossed spit-balls or paper airplanes to each other. They also stared at the ceiling, bored out of their minds, waiting for the bell to ring. Loafing in the old days usually meant doing nothing. Today, students are busier than ever, but are not necessarily engaged in activities that lead to making progress to the head of the class.

I have outlined some activities below that distract students from studying. Check this list out. You will recognize some typical behaviors:

- Plugging ears to MP3 players and iPods
- Receiving and sending text messages
- Watching movies online
- Chatting on cell phones
- Playing video games
- Going on Facebook and other social media sites
- Surfing the 'net
- Fake studying
- Hanging out
- Posturing
- Snoozing
- Sexting
- Flirting
- Tweeting
- Cramming
- Goofing off
- Daydreaming

"Anything and everything but study in study hall" is the way my colleague, Shawn Surber, describes it. I am sure you can add to the list. I hope you will replace this waste-of-time list with proactive steps to success.

Resting in the Library While Reading in Bed: What's wrong with this Picture?

Besides study hall, other free time venues provide perfect opportunities for studying in which 'busy-loafing' activities derail the quest to excel. When libraries are not used for study, they often become centers for meeting friends, texting, and chillin', as one student described it to me. In some cases, parents ask their children to wait for them in the library after school. The library becomes a waiting station for a new generation of 'latch-key kids' or a hangout for bored students to do some 'busy-loafing' with high-tech toys as previously described. It seldom occurs to library staff to do much more than demand silence and teachers do not always provide instructions on how to get the most out of regular visits to the library.

College students may be tempted to view the library as a quiet, soothing place of escape. The study cubicles beckon the weary to lay their heads in a repose mode instead of a study mode.

There is a big irony in all of this. When students waste precious time loafing in the place of study, they end up needing to study in a place of rest. A bed is for sleeping, not for studying, cramming or doing required reading. To lie in bed with a book or set of notes by one's side is to pit the desire to rest squarely against the need to be mentally alert to tackle abstract ideas. Placing a book in your hand to be stared at with eyes that have been deactivated as part of the brain's mental alertness shutdown program spells disaster. Sleep usually wins out. Why should anyone expect otherwise when the body has been given orders to quit thinking and start snoozing?

The habit of studying in bed is ineffective and must be stopped. It wastes valuable study time and creates anxiety. By the time you want to catch up, it's too late. The time has been spent.

J.K. Rowling, the author of the Harry Potter series, reveals how time does not slow down for you: "It's a strange thing, but when you are dreading something, and would give anything to slow down time, it has a disobliging habit of speeding up."

The kitchen, dinner table, living room, recreation area, bathroom and bedroom all serve specific primary functions. Our bodies are predisposed to the stimulation suggested by those primary functions. What is the right recipe for studying effectively? Students need a proper space for study; an uncluttered, quiet and calm environment. A comfortable chair, good lighting, notes with clear directions from the teacher and a rested spirit do wonders to help you read, absorb, analyze and understand your assignments. It also helps to team up with someone like you, striving to excel.

Listening to Music While Studying:
Friend or Foe?

Then, there is music. Will your favorite music do well in setting moods that resonate with your need to concentrate on your studies? While some people like studying with music in the background, it has the potential to emotionally catapult you to another place and time. When musical sounds and lyrics create moods that derail your concentration, you are shooting yourself in the foot. You will not be able to focus on studying if you have soulful love songs tugging at your emotions, stimulating sensual feelings or reminding you of being jilted or abandoned.

The same goes for rhythmic music that sets feet tapping, hips swinging or makes you want to sing! Hip hop, country, Latin, Indian pop, classical, alternative, rock and even religious music are all genres that will incite reactions you may find yourself trying to manage when you should be studying. I caution you to choose your music carefully. Find out how music will affect you before you decide to turn it on while doing your studies.

The arrivals of MP3 players and iPods have allowed students to collect and organize their favorite sounds and plug them in their ears, making the music factor a potentially huge challenge. This music has its time and place, but not always during your study time. Put an end to distractive noises. Your mind has to think about what you are studying.

Sounds that are perfectly suited for fun, celebration or getting psyched up for a night out may collide head on with the need for mental clarity.

Students from across the country and international destinations are having their say in diverse Internet venues, like blogs. Their opinions resonate with those in search of answers to the important question: Will listening to music in a place of study prove to be a help or a hindrance?

Interested in what students have to say, I started to eavesdrop on the conversations between bloggers on the topic. Here are a couple of excerpts from their exchanges:

"It's so weird, but I can listen to music only while doing math, but can't if it involves reading."

Another student put it this way: "Listening to music doesn't affect my concentration perceptibly while doing homework, but it probably has a detrimental effect upon its quality."

The Risks of Distractions or Taking a Vacation from Learning

The same principle applies to any stimulation of the senses, like video games, computers, sports programs, sitcoms, reality shows, cartoons, movies, and ads. These media products have but one goal in mind, to capture your undivided attention and keep you away from the competition. The real danger is when studying becomes the competition.

What you need to appreciate is that while educational programs are often presented in boring, passive frameworks, they are more important to concentrate on right now if you want to enjoy well-earned leisure later on. Success as a competent member of the workforce, a responsible citizen and a healthy human being is linked to the exercise of discipline.

In other words, learning to get rid of highly ineffective study habits prepares you for this success. Every obstacle that detracts from your journey towards educational success must be avoided. My advice is simple. Seize study time for study. You must stop loafing, start learning and exercise self-discipline. Now is the time to jump-start, leap-frog and catapult yourself to the head of the class!

School teacher Gail Salvato points out, "When the children come back in the fall, if they have not been reading in summer, you usually do see a decline."

Never take a vacation from learning. The break periods between semesters and academic years provide willing learners with wonderful opportunities for continued growth. Keep your mental muscles exercised. Build your vocabulary skills through reading. Make use of the dictionary. Join a reading or discussion group. If one is not established in your community, start one. Be prepared to reconnect with your learning adventure by having a strong, informed and engaged mind in the world of ideas. Do not waste these long breaks by taking a leave of absence from learning. Eva Young cautions, "To think too long about doing a thing often becomes its undoing." So, don't think about studying, just do it!

Why Some Students Keep Learning During the Long Summer Break

Bear in mind that many of the students from middle-class families, where reading is nurtured, never stop reading, even during summer breaks. They continue to increase their vocabulary and position themselves to enter the new school year already mentally alert. That's because they have parents who make sure of that.

Ron Fairchild put it this way, "For some children, summer vacation means camp, family trips, visits to museums, parks and libraries and a variety of enriching activities."

But if you do not have those resources, you must take steps to ensure that the long summer breaks are not for loafing. They are a time for continual learning, especially through the joy of reading, reading and more reading. When you discipline yourself to stay focused on your quest for knowledge, you have learned the greatest lesson of all - you have learned to learn!

Read memoirs and biographies. They are fun and full of information. For example, if you want to become an educator in the hood/barrio, you may want to read the book by Rafe Esquith, Teach like Your Hair Was on Fire! He is totally committed to his students' success.

If you are interested in civil rights law, consider reading Vernon Can Read. Vernon Jordan, the author, describes his journey of removing the racial barriers that had to be torn down before Barack Obama could become the president of the United States.

The book by Chi Fa La with Becky White, Double Luck: The Memoir of a Chinese Orphan is inspirational. The memoir traces the journey of an unwanted child from China to England and finally to the US, and how she bounces back from adversity and triumphs in becoming a doctor.

Another book for young people is by Linda Sue Park, When My Name Was Keoko. The memoir is about a young Korean during the 1940s under Japanese occupation. Please Stop Laughing at Me: One Woman's Inspirational Story, by Jodee Blanco, reveals how it feels to be bullied in school. When I was Puerto Rican, by Esmeralda Santiago, speaks of the adventure of a bilingual journey of a young Latina. The book by Bill Strickland, Making the Impossible, Possible, just blew me away. He went from being a mediocre student in the poor neighborhoods of Pittsburg to an awesome social entrepreneur. I have recently read the book by a very resilient Somali woman, Waris Dirie, called Desert Flower. Are you interested, for example, in becoming a health professional? Then, Google the question, "What are the best books about the health professions?" Presto, a list of books becomes available at your fingertips.

Do not waste time! Keep your mind alive, engaged and excited about learning. Read for yourself, not for others. Reading books that feed your personal hunger to make a difference in society, help you understand the world and most important, increase your competencies.

STRATEGIES FOR SUCCESS

All great achievements require time.

Maya Angelou

a) Deepen your faith plus gain a study-competitive advantage on weekends.

Wake up early. Embrace the days you have off from school. Put first things first. If you have weekend traditions for worship and fulfilling sacred obligations that hold community and family together, then you should definitely honor those.

There is wisdom in setting some time on a weekly basis for spiritual nourishment. Do not sleep in when you should be engaged at a synagogue, temple, mosque, church or community center. You can expand your vocabulary and world view by reading exciting books related to the journey of the heroic icons of your faith.

Emulate their triumphs. Learn to live a purpose-driven life. Make sure you grow socially, physically, intellectually and, if it matters to you personally, spiritually. There is too much greed, hatred and violence in the world. A spiritual life grounds you in values, keeps you focused, and can provide a meaningful content for caring about yourself and those around you.

Once you have satisfied your spiritual requirements, do your homework! Don't wait until Sunday night when your energies are spent. You will likely suffer the consequences. You may even lose the opportunity for meaningful collaborations with peers and adults to help with your homework assignments. Having fun to celebrate your academic achievements is far better than having to cram because you failed to use the weekend wisely.

Outstanding championship games can be recorded and watched later as a reward for putting first things first. Do not waste time glued to the set. Watch the highlights, if you must. Why settle for being a bystander who watches champions perform when you can study to become a champion yourself! Joseph Joubert said, "Genius begins great works; labor alone finishes them."

b) Become engaged in educational activities to prevent summer learning loss.

Let us take a second look at the urgent issue of summer learning loss. Don't be so quick to embrace the notion, "When the school year ends, the fun begins." Studies reveal that during the long summer break, some students lose a great deal of what they learned during the regular school year.

Ron Fairchild, who directs the Johns Hopkins University Center for Summer Learning, found that, "All students experience summer learning losses when they're not engaged in constructive educational learning opportunities."

Dr. Ruth Peter in her article, "Preventing Summer Learning Loss," added, "On average, students lose approximately 2.5 months of grade level equivalency in mathematical computation skills during the summer months. Low income children and youth experience greater summer learning losses than their higher-income peers."

So there you have it. If you snooze during the summer break, you will lose academic ground.

Let the fun of summer begin and end with reading books that inspire, inform and increase your understanding of complex issues.

My mentor taught me that time off from school was ideal for self-initiated reading of 25 pages a day. That was when I was working full-time. Consider reading 50 pages a day. My thirteen-year-old granddaughter says, "That is perfectly doable!"

My mentor taught me to choose memoirs and read them carefully. I was instructed to use my dictionary as a way of empowering myself with new words. If my parents could not read to me, then it was my responsibility to read to myself. I discovered that the summer break was the perfect time to anticipate the books that were going to be required in the next grade, so I got a head start by reading some of them.

I learned rather late in my academic journey that, even without the parental support middle-class children enjoy, you do not have to lose ground during the summer and other school breaks. Join formal programs that will increase your knowledge about issues that are vital to your growth. Camps, official tours of museums and reading groups can be fun and full of insights.

c) Sprint forward during holiday breaks.

Have fun during holiday breaks. Enjoy family celebrations. Participate in sacred traditions. However, do not squander your study-bonus opportunities. Use this time to complete school work. Read ahead. Anticipate future requirements. Get together with students who have already taken your classes and seek their advice on what is likely to come up next. Learn to network with like-minded classmates on how to use your holiday periods wisely. Use technology to communicate with your learning partners. Enlist the support of family members. Engage them in helping you to stay focused.

Spending time with loved ones during these festive occasions may provide special opportunities for learning valuable lessons about life. My older brother died an alcoholic. In a sober moment during a family gathering, he confided in me, "If I had known that I would live this long, I would have taken much better care of my body." Do you take care of your body? Are you messing with legal or illegal drugs likely to derail your health and great purposes in life? Are you eating the wrong kinds of foods and wasting away? Even from my brother's troubled journey, I had something to learn.

Learn what to avoid from family members who wish they could have done things differently. Corner the successful members of your family and engage them in a discussion on how they were able to excel. Find private time for reflection and advice. Listen to what they have to say about the skill sets you should develop in school for becoming a productive member of work teams.

d) Get close to the right books and stay away from the wrong people.

People are wrong for you if they are not living meaningful lives. If they do not value education, they will value the things that will put you at risk. Avoid squandering your time or dignity by hanging out with people without vision or purpose. You know who they are. Befriend people who are in conflict with mediocrity, engaged in improving themselves and making their communities better. These types of friends are valuable to your quest. Laugh, play and read with them.

Walk with authors who got it wrong and fixed it. They will share a road map in their memoirs that will assist you in your own journey to excel. Mary Yamazaki, my mentor and guide, made me realize that by reading great books, I would never have to walk alone.

I befriended the authors of the autobiographies, biographies and memoirs, which I read. In doing so, I soon realized I did not have to hang out with losers or waste valuable time watching mindless TV programs.

Reading allowed me to walk with giants of history and people who reinvented themselves through adversity. I could find inspiration in the triumphs of others. Although I read alone, I was never lonely.

GETTING IT RIGHT CASE STUDY

Don't say you don't have enough time. You have
exactly the same number of hours per day that
were given to Helen Keller, Pasteur,
Michelangelo, Mother Teresa, Leonardo de Vinci,
Thomas Jefferson and Albert Einstein.

H. Jackson Brown

My name is Carlos Jiménez Flores. I have a
Bachelor's degree in Human Resource
Development, with a minor in Sociology. I have
published several books and have produced and
directed several feature films. Yet, my successes
do not reflect the academic hardships, struggles
and obstacles I had to overcome in order to
accomplish something.

My study habits were forged early on at the
elementary school level. Unfortunately, they were
bad. When my family moved to the United States,
we did not speak English. I did not have anybody
at home who could help me with homework.

I did not have any friends or relatives who could
come over to help. I did not belong to any study
group made up of peers since I did not make
those connections in school. Consequently, I was
left alone to fend for myself.

Going solo is what I knew. I did my best to
complete the tasks given to me at Christopher
Columbus Elementary School. Whatever

instruction I did not understand, I simply ignored. The unfinished homework would get done the next day by copying from another student or I just straightforwardly did not do it. This was my modus operandi until I learned English.

Once I learned English, my grades improved. I was an honor student in Puerto Rico while attending a school named Felipe Gutierrez in the town of Río Piedras. I knew I could succeed. However, I was still doing it wrong. I was still going solo; no study groups. What I did not understand, I merely passed over.

I was still cheating by copying answers from my friends. I asked my father to build a desk for me so I may study and he did. Sadly, the desk was in the living room and the television was always on, so I could not concentrate. I retreated to my bedroom and my bed became my desk.

It took me a couple of years, but I finally came into my own. I was succeeding academically. I made the honor roll. I stopped cheating by copying from my friends. Just when I was getting into the groove of things, my mother (who was now divorced) decided to enroll my sister and I in a private school, St. Hedwig. My mother's decision was based on safety, not on academics. She was afraid that I would succumb to the violent, gang-infested, drug-ridden world we were living in.

So here I am, starting all over again. New school; I did not have any friends, but at least I spoke the language. I quickly realized that I was behind academically. There was a big gap between private and public education and I had just become its latest victim. I was trying to keep up, yet I was drowning. I was completely unprepared and my survival instincts kicked in. I resorted to my old modus operandi. Whatever instruction I did not understand, I simply ignored.

I became an average student at that private school. Making the honor roll was beyond my reach. I was good enough to pass, not bad enough to fail.

I spent the three years at that school in the middle of the pack. I was always playing catch-up, seemingly viewed as mediocre by peers and faculty. My study habits were horrendous. I studied alone all the time. If I studied in the living room, it was with the television on. If I studied in my bedroom, it was lying on my bed with the stereo on.

I went to a public high school with my study habits intact. Surprisingly, I found my first two years, freshman and sophomore, to be extremely easy at William H. Wells High School. The unbalanced difference between a private and public school education reared its head again. However, this time around it was in my favor. I was essentially repeating what had been covered in private school during seventh and eighth grade at the public high school. My first two years of high school, I had a 3.9 grade point average and became the Salutatorian of my class during that span.

I was academically ranked as number two in a class of nearly a thousand students.

This was the worst situation that could have happened. I already had bad study habits. Now, I was getting A's without having to study. I was acing exams simply because I already had learned the material in elementary school.

High school was simply not challenging. I became bored. For the first time, I began cutting class. I stopped doing homework. There was no need to do homework if I was getting A's on the exams. I used study periods to hang out, loaf around. I engaged peers in the same destructive behaviors, except my grades were not reflective of my habits and delinquency.

It would finally catch up to me my junior and senior years, when I transferred to another public high school, Roberto Clemente Community Academy, in order to play baseball for them. No longer able to ride on previously learned material at the elementary level, I quickly found myself drowning academically once more. I was doing homework and studying again, but I was doing it solo. The stereo or television or both would be blaring. I started another bad study habit.

I waited until the night before to study for an exam. I was still cutting class and I was still goofing around during study hall periods. My grades were dipping fast those last two years of high school. I eventually graduated. My report card was very reflective of my bad study habits and behavior. I graduated with D's and F's.

I entered college, bringing along with me my arsenal of bad habits and behaviors, which included studying alone, not showing up (cutting class), studying with the television on, hanging out in the places of study (i.e., library, designated study areas), studying with music on, going to class without having read assigned chapters or articles, goofing off in class/not paying attention, not completing homework assignments, and when I did, it was turned in late. I was also an expert crammer.

To make matters worse, I found like-minded peers on campus at Northeastern Illinois University. Our spot was near the bookstore. There was a seating section that was shaped in a square, eight by eight feet. It had seat cushions all around and the center was wood. Our group had about twenty core members. It was not a study group.

We would have other students come and hang from time to time. We used the middle wooden area for our bags, coats and books.

With our clique being Latino, we called the area we sat in the Bochinche Box. Bochinche means "gossip" in Spanish. Box, because the seating area was square.

We would hang out there Monday through Thursday 8a.m. - 2p.m., which was when the majority of us attended the university. No one was ever late.

At any given time, there would at least be 10 of us hanging out at the Bochinche Box. Most times we went to class, although there also was a lot of skipping class. Aside from the gossiping, there was a lot of just hanging out. Not a lot of activity. Just sitting around, cracking jokes, playing around, planning our evenings and weekends.

We would also bring liquor on campus. Our university is a commuter college. So the girls would bring liquor in their purses, the guys would bring their liquor in their backpacks. Usually at the end of the day, we would go in a group to a nearby restaurant to eat and hang some more or we would go to someone's house and party.

To party would mean drink liquor, do drugs and just hang out.

Sex was also a factor in our interactions. Some of the guys were dating some of the girls. Some in the group hooked up and were having casual sex. Out of all the fooling around, one couple did marry.

Eventually, the Bochinche Box disbanded. Most dropped out, including me. Not many stayed behind. Those who did, graduated and earned their degrees. Most of the ones who dropped out have not gone back. A handful returned. I am one of them.

It was not easy. In order to succeed, I understood I had to do away with old habits and behaviors. I developed a relationship with a former professor who agreed to mentor me. I was rewired, reprogrammed. It was a new me. I knew the right thing to do was to go to college. I just did not know how to do the right thing right. However, I was given a blueprint by my mentor, Dr. Samuel Betances; someone who had been there, someone with a similar background as mine, someone who had succeeded, someone who went from the 'hood to Harvard.

No more cramming for me. I read all material in a timely manner and highlighted all the major points. I did all of my homework. No more hanging out. I exchanged contact information with the top students of every class I had. I formed study groups. I no longer did it alone. I took copious notes in class. I even highlighted the important points in my notes.

I never missed a class just for the sake of missing a class. I was done with partying.

When I was not studying with a group, I was either in the library or at home (without the television on or music playing) at my desk. I even sought tutoring at the university whenever I needed it. And it was free! Imagine that. I was focused. My days of loafing in the places of study were long gone. My mission was to succeed at a high level.

Mission accomplished. I graduated with high honors from Wilbur Wright Community College while earning my Associates degree. I was on the Dean's List. I am a member of Phi Theta Kappa, which is the International Honor Society of Two-Year Colleges. I took honors courses and graduated from the same institution of higher learning I had dropped out of years earlier, earning a Bachelor's degree at Northeastern Illinois University.

I had come full circle.

CONCLUSION

Don't loaf in the places of study and don't study in the places for loafing. Carlos Jimenez found that he had to replace bad study habits with good ones. He came to me for guidance, but he was prepared to listen, follow advice and take steps to excel. He turned his fortunes around and increased his competencies as a student. You can do the same. There are caring adults in your networks waiting for a signal from you to assist your climb to the head of the class. Don't disappoint them—your future depends on it!

Let the summer fun begin by deciding which books you will read to make your spirits soar. Choose from the many lists for young readers you can access on the Internet. Ask people who have excelled what books they recommend.

Enjoy learning, growing in wisdom and claiming the authors as your friends. Don't let unfamiliar words escape as strangers – get to know them and welcome them as companions for your life of learning and communicating.

If you don't read and expand your intellect during the summer and vacation breaks, you will lose academic ground.

STEP 6

Study with All of Your Senses, Some Classmates and Trusted Guides

None of us is as smart as all of us.

Ken Blanchard

WHY YOU MUST GET IT RIGHT!

Don't make studying a solitary, one-dimensional endeavor. Use all of your senses and collaborate with like-minded peers. Studying in groups is particularly useful as small group discussions multiply learning. The more learning tools you utilize, the better the results.

You must seek the wisdom of your trusted guides to give you advice, feedback and technical assistance. Capitalize on learning from their competencies and skills to aid in your endeavors. Completing graduation requirements with the help of these resources is just plain smart.

Study with All of Your Senses

"Quiet on the set!" is a familiar director's

command in Hollywood film lots. It's followed by, "Lights, camera, action!" Then the acting begins in earnest. Scenes with dialogue and drama unfold and the story is pieced together. They will be framed by music, special effects and credits into a film product that will be released into theaters, video stores and TV venues.

Filmmaking is scripted. Nothing is left to chance. Diverse resources are artistically leveraged on the set and finalized in studios. Film directors do their best work by guiding cast members and technical teams to harmoniously interact and do their magic before the cameras. Audiences get to enjoy the fruits of those labors on the big screen. That, in a nutshell, is how filmmaking works. The process is full of lessons for students.

To excel at studying, you must direct your senses to capture in your mind what is worth knowing in the same way that film directors capture on camera what is worth showing.

In order to create magic in the classroom, you must study differently. You should practice placing information in three different parts of your memory bank – seeing it, saying it and hearing it.

To produce academic excellence, you must start by directing your senses to the task in ways that emulate the filmmaker's craft. You must be multi-dimensional in your study approach. Summon all of your senses to the study lot. Make sure all of them are prepared to play their part. Insist on quiet. Claim the space for the drama, reading and dialogue that will follow. You are about to direct and produce a great scene in your victory over ignorance story. Your voice, eyes, ears and hands will all play a key part. Your brain will retain vital information to be shared in critical discussions and exams in the auditoriums and stages of schools, where the memorized scripts can then be shared with critics and evaluators.

You heard me say that small group discussions multiply learning. Well, short of that, activating multiple senses to focus on what must be learned is the next best thing. While you shouldn't study alone, when that kind of networking is not possible, find a quiet place where you can use all of your senses to get better study results.

Engage Your Senses by Reading Out Loud

There are several ways of reading. When your goal is to master materials that must be put to memory for tests or presentations, consider reading out loud. This method allows you to play the roles of both speaker and listener. Reading out loud clearly illustrates how the multi–dimensional use of senses adds value to study outcomes.

Engaging your senses in this way makes the learning experience fun, spirited and memorable. Consider advice offered by Dean Papadopoulos, "Why not read standing as you employ the drama of storytelling and dialogue and narrative and volume and gaze and gesture and facial expressions and sounds (tone) to communicate what the author intends to communicate, but needs your active participation to do so since the paper and ink can't do it for you?"

Reading out loud has the potential for substantially increasing your retention rate. The interactions between your eyes as you read, your voice as you pronounce words into sentences, your ears as you hear what is written, and your brain which processes and synthesizes what your senses absorb, will strengthen concepts, deepen comprehension and improve your ability to recall the information at a later time. Reading out loud was especially effective for me.

I encourage you to get intellectually creative and have fun by becoming theatrical about reading out loud. To improve your ability to retain the information you read, try teaching the most significant lessons in a loud voice to yourself. This may seem silly at first, but trust me, it works.

Let's pretend your name is Erin. Call yourself to attention. Address yourself with authority. Raise your voice in the spirit of a caring teacher or parent. Say, "Listen up, Erin. There are three very important conclusions in this chapter. They are, one… and two… and three…" Afterwards, check it out. Consult your notes or the text to see if you were on point. If not, do it again. The second time around, you will be more accurate. Say to yourself, "Erin, you had only two correct answers.

The third was incomplete. Here is what the author says is the right conclusion…" That's right. You are re-reading and teaching yourself out loud in the spirit of a real educational encounter.

Douglas Jobes, in an article entitled "Improve Your Memory by Using All Your Senses," encourages students to use the 'whole brain' to remember things better. He offers 10 steps for remembering new materials:

1) See it!
2) Say it!
3) Write it!
4) Do it!
5) Draw it!
6) Imagine it!
7) Research it!
8) Emotionalize it!
9) Convert it!
10) Question it!

Log on to SelfGrowth.com to learn more about how you can engage more sensory pathways to help you jog your memory with useful information needed for your educational journey.

Reading Out Loud Improves
Your Writing and Language Learning Skills

Reading out loud has other benefits. It will sharpen your writing and improve your language learning skills as well. Let's focus on writing skills first.

James Chartrand in his Blog, Men with Pen, reminds us that, "Writing requires that you keep in mind the reader of your written text. Reading aloud is a valuable exercise to improve your writing. Your words become crystal clear and they'll convey a more powerful, effective message that gets you better results. Here's why: You'll spot paragraphs that end abruptly. You'll notice transitions between ideas aren't as smooth as you thought they were. You'll hear if your introduction sounds weak or choppy and you'll discover whether your wrap-up encourages conversation or just stops it cold."

By hearing what you've written, you can identify areas needing improvement. I am sure you have had the experience where you've paused when writing a letter or note to muse to yourself that "something just doesn't sound right."

Chartrand goes on to say that, "You can rework your writing and nip all the awkwardness so that you create flow between paragraphs, clarify your ideas, expand on skimpy sections and hone the perfect lead-in and wrap-up. Read it aloud once more, give it a last polish and voila, excellence!"

Let's look at how this strategy can also facilitate language learning. In his article, "Why Reading Out Loud is Vital," Jeff Gregory, who is the World Languages Lab Coordinator at El Centro College, makes the business case that you can increase retention of information by 100 percent by reading out loud.

Chances are that most of you live in a home where a target language - the language you may be trying to learn (whether it be English as your second language, middle-class English proficiency, or a foreign language) - is not spoken. You must therefore create opportunities to practice speaking your target language. One way you can do this is to read the language out loud in your home. When you read silently, you use just two parts of your body. You guessed it – brain and eyes. But when you read out loud, you use four parts of your body - brain, eyes, ears and voice. Retention is significantly improved. You not only think about the language and see it written; you speak and hear it as well.

Claim your area of study and transform it into a private theater to unleash all of your senses. Let your voice fill your study space. This will help you to incorporate your target language into your thinking and speech patterns.

Papadopoulos is on point again: "So make the ideas come alive, make the story come alive, make your imagination come alive and marshal all the senses available to you in your blessed being to learn fully what is meant to be learned."

Become your own best director by activating your senses to play key roles in your real life educational drama. Don't be a passive learner. Give the command, "Quiet on the set; Lights, camera, action!" And, let the award-winning story of your successful journey to the head of the class continue to unfold.

Study with Some of Your Classmates

Some students claim they study alone and still excel in school. While they appear to be self-reliant, a closer look shows that they have a vast network of support to back them up. In other words, their experiences have prepared them for academic success. Access to resources at home and, through family and friendship circles, has taught them how to navigate the route to the head of the class and avoid pitfalls.

They learn how to study, are equipped with a healthy vocabulary and march to the tune of high expectations from their teachers. When a problem arises, assistance is readily available. This may not be the case for you, especially if you come from a family where your parents have not graduated from high school or college.

You must not travel alone on your road to academic excellence. Team up with students who are respected as the "real deal" by the teachers. They are easy to spot. Take note of who pays attention, asks questions, participates in discussions, takes copious notes, pre-reads the assignments and voices informed opinions.

Once you have identified classmates who are hungry to matter and eager to learn, introduce yourself and invite them to form a study group for the duration of the course. Avoid making the group an exclusive club for the 'smart students.' Strike a balance between students who know a lot about the subject and those who do not. The benefits and values of the discussions that take place across generations of learners will be huge.

Some students have found that studying with others is a disaster!

Too much fooling around and off-topic conversations sidetrack the main objective. Recruit only serious-minded students. It can be a waste of time otherwise.

When studying, you really need to understand and recall important ideas. The best way to learn and remember is to share, compare and review lessons being learned with others. While engaged in study, the human mind has to separate solid ideas from weak or vague ones. The mind does this best through dialogue and collaboration. Learning takes root when others, who have your best interests at heart, challenge your assumptions, seek insights, give feedback, correct errors, press for consistency, add value by sharing illustrations and provide alternative perspectives.

Studying in groups is a dynamic process that works, provided all members of the study group show up prepared for a fruitful exchange after having done their share of the preparatory work.

I recently read a comment on a blog about study groups. One student made a key observation: "To benefit from group study, you really need to study on your own first. Get a grasp of the basic facts and then use your peers to discuss and debate ideas."

There is wisdom in listening to students who have benefitted from the process. They are clear about the pitfalls of using study groups as socializing sessions. If you take safeguards and team up with those who are equally committed, you will excel.

Do not acquiesce to the notion that you can substitute face-to-face interactions with a chat room over the Internet to accomplish the goal of the study group. The face-to-face real-time contact is crucial for growing academically in a study group.

Agree on a meeting protocol: all are required to read assignments and take notes before discussing issues; no one speaks twice until everyone speaks once, etc... Give everyone in the group an opportunity to facilitate a session.

Students who coast and do not come prepared to add value to the team should forfeit their membership in the study group. The worst thing is to milk the thinking of others without contributing. Study teams must not be corrupted by procrastinators! By doing their fair share of the work, team members will dutifully help the other participants step up to the head of the class.

When You Tutor Others, You Learn More

Tutors learn a lot more than the people they tutor. When you explain something to someone else, it becomes clearer in your own mind. The reason why teachers tend to know a great deal more than students is due in part to their constantly engaging, challenging, explaining and sharing knowledge with new generations of students. The more a teacher tries to explain something in ways that diverse learners can grasp, the more the teacher learns! You, too, can deepen your comprehension by explaining what you have learned to others.

Sandra Tattershall wrote about the benefits that will come your way when you agree to help others, "The tutors learning more is not surprising when one considers the tutor must be active in explaining the concept or process in question… In trying to make something clear, the tutor tests their own knowledge. They discover what they really understand and what they need to know."

If you want to discover what you really know and 'sharpen your saw' while you increase your knowledge, become a tutor. Don't study solo. Study with a classmate who needs your help. In the process, you will learn more than the student you are helping.

Seek Guidance from Adults Rich in Social Capital

Social capital relates to how some people gain more success in a particular setting through their extensive networks. Through their observations and superior connections, adults who are rich in social capital know how to connect the dots. They are well-to-do people who "know the ropes," so to speak, and can assist you in understanding how to get educated and graduate from complex, demanding, rigorous places of learning. You need to find caring adults who are wise and generous and can guide your success by leveraging their social capital.

Learning how to study is not easy. Knowing how to do research can be daunting. Getting feedback on whether an essay is clear and precise is essential. Working hard and not making progress can be disappointing. Deciding what career track to follow after high school will be difficult. How to deal with a difficult teacher requires skill. You can benefit greatly from having a caring adult with social capital who shares knowledge, strategies and wisdom from their life experiences, to help you make the best decisions. You don't have to re-invent the wheel.

Seriously consider the sound advice offered by Cesar Chavez: "You are never strong enough that you don't need help." If loved ones do not have the social capital necessary for assisting you to become educated and graduate from school, you must actively seek out a member of your community with social capital. For example, you may want to approach an educator to take on the role of coach and mentor. I turned to my history teacher in college. He helped me become strong. Who will you turn to?

Find people and persuade them that you are the real deal. Recruit them to guide you. Doing so is essential for your journey to the head of the class. Always show respect in the way you provide feedback to those who invest in you.

Remember, you are not replacing the support from your loved ones; you are growing your networks in order to excel. If your loved ones understand the value of education, they will applaud you. If not, they will learn over time why getting an education before settling down to work full time is the smart and right thing to do.

There are three things you must keep in mind as you expand your own social capital:

- First, don't be upset with your parents for not giving you what they do not have. Honor them for bringing you into the world and sending you to school. You don't have to feel guilty for seeking counsel and guidance from other caring adults. You are not betraying your parents. Quite the contrary, you are laying the pathway to success for younger siblings and relatives in your family network. I was able to financially assist my parents in their old age because I graduated from college and achieved professional status and income through the help of caring adults who mentored me. Honor your loved ones by reaching out to caring adults who are not related to you by bloodlines, but through great purposes that can only be achieved through education.

- Second, realize that the adults you seek to mentor you, will do so out of their own desire to contribute. They will not be put off or offended by the request. Caring adults with social capital are eager to be of service to a passionate student who has fire in the belly, is hungry to matter and eager to learn. They find joy and fulfillment in being asked to do something of value on behalf of an emerging educated professional.

- Finally, you must demonstrate a profound respect for the generosity of these adults by communicating with them in a timely fashion. Live up to what you agree to do from one session to the next. Give feedback at the conclusion of each encounter and go over what you now understand compared to when you first started. As soon as you get the chance, write a brief note of gratitude with a list of the to-dos before the next meeting. This is a signal to your guide that you are serious about growing your talents by leveraging the social capital of caring adults.

Pluses Can Equal Minuses in the Absence of Social Capital

My mother loved me. I was her fat little boy and she named me Samuel after a prophet in the Bible. She had very high hopes for me. However, she became a single parent and could not take care of my brothers and me. She took us to Puerto Rico and entrusted us to people who needed errand boys in exchange for room and board. We were separated for a few years. When she finally sent for us, she was living in the Bronx.

Although I was required to go to school, I could not understand any English, so I depended on my friend, Victor, who knew both Spanish and English, to be my translator. Miss Harmel taught several subjects, including arithmetic. Even the most basic math concepts were new to me. She worked hard and called on students, who raised their hands to show off their mastery of what they had been taught. I missed out on the explanations. I was smart. But, I did not know how to learn in English, so Victor broke it down for me. He told me that I had to do fourteen problems in the book for homework.

After supper, I began this feat. Even though I worked hard, it was no use. The first problem was wrong and I knew it. Then the second and third; by the time I had completed the fourth, I was practically in tears. My mama passed by and saw me stressed out and sad. She picked me up and sat me in the safest place on the whole earth - her lap.

"I have to do fourteen arithmetic problems," I explained. "The first four, I did. But I know that they are wrong. I have to do ten more and I don't know how!"

"My son, don't worry. I am going to help you."

I smiled and felt better already. She picked up a yellow #2 pencil, wet it with the tip of her tongue and began to work in earnest. I remember she struggled with that problem for the longest time. After deliberating, she finally leaned back and said, "There." Problem number five was done. I kissed her. She did problem numbers six, seven and eight. I kissed her again and again and again. We were on a roll. She was doing the problems and I was doing the kissing. I loved it. She did all ten problems. I then proceeded to copy all of them in my own handwriting. The next day, I proudly handed in my homework.

Two days later, the homework papers were returned. Miss Harmel had a habit of folding them in half so we could carefully open them at our own discretion. I opened mine slowly. Sure enough, the first four I had done had big red X's after each problem. I expected that. I knew they were wrong. Then, to my surprise, the ten my mama had done had ten red X's! I could not believe it. I was dumbfounded.

There had to be some mistake, so I rushed over

to Victor and showed him the horrible miscarriage of justice that the teacher had committed.

"Victor, Victor, come here. Look at this," I hurriedly pointed out in Spanish.

"What's going on?"

"I'll tell you what's going on. Miss Harmel marked all of my problems wrong!! Look at all these red X's. Look."

"Well, it looks like you didn't do them right..."

"No, no. You don't understand. I did the first four. I know those are wrong. But what Miss Harmel does not know is that my mama did the next ten! And she marked them all wrong... that ain't right!!" I protested.

"Calm down, little brother, calm down..." Victor's light went on. He finally had something on Miss Harmel. He was going to expose her. And I gave him the ammunition to do it with. It was now between Victor and Miss Harmel.

It couldn't have worked out better than if I had planned it myself, I thought.

He took my paper and we walked up to her desk. He explained that Sammy got some bad news he did not deserve. He broke it down like lawyers did in the movies.

"Miss Harmel, Sammy has a confession to make. See his paper. The first four he did. And he knows that those are wrong." He deliberately paused. It was a set up.

Victor was licking his chops. He had her where he wanted her. "But what you don't know is that his mama did the next ten – and you marked them all wrong!" It was a done deal, she had been exposed.

Victor crossed his hands and waited for her to stammer, apologize and make amends. He was about to win his first big case, and he was only in the fourth grade.

She stood up. It was rebuttal time. She looked carefully at the evidence, put the paper down and spoke calmly in a very deliberate tone, "You tell Sammy, that his mother does not know what she is doing!"

Victor turned to me and told me what she said. She said something about my mama, I fumed. So, I said something about her mama. And, stupid Victor translated it. That's how I met my first principal. I ended up writing something on the blackboard 500 times as punishment. To this day, I don't know what I wrote. It was in English. Nonetheless, I learned two lessons that day. One, don't ever say anything about a teacher's mama. Two, if you get help from people who mean well but don't know any more than you do, you will fail.

I often think about the challenge that students from poverty face. Like me, they have loving parents, hardworking teachers and are very smart to boot. Three big plusses if you ask me. However, in the end, those plusses can equal minuses. I can attest to that from my own experience!

Without help from caring adults with social capital, failure promises to be a predictable outcome. My mother loved me, but could not give me what she did not have. My success in school came by the incredibly good fortune of finding caring adults who mentored me into becoming a successful student. Even my peers made a positive difference. Don't study solo. Collaborate with your peers and caring adults who have your best interest and success at heart.

STRATEGIES FOR SUCCESS

When you explain your reasoning aloud, gaps and mistakes quickly appear, and you (and your fellow group members) can quickly correct your reasoning. Taking turns in explaining difficult material helps build confidence in all the members.

Avi Cohen

a) Make new friends in study groups.

Joining or creating a study group is a great way to make new friends. If you become part of a sports team or a theater cast, you will find that practice and rehearsals bond the team members into a circle of trust. If you study in groups, you can gain that important benefit of receiving immediate, affirming feedback from team members. The diversity of thought generated by team members in the exchange of ideas and perspectives enriches the learning adventure for all.

In a mission-driven study group, you simply cannot let your team members down. Discussions have a way of triggering ideas that energize analysis and complex thinking. The rush you get from reaching the top level in a video game pales in comparison to knowing that, with your help, a classmate solved a puzzle that improved his or her academic performance. Helping others is good for your own sense of worth. Your self-esteem will soar.

b) Engage with other students who are the real deal.

At the beginning of the semester, assess which students are serious learners.

They are easy to spot - they refuse to be distracted, sit toward the front, come prepared, actively participate, and take copious notes. Approach one or more of them and tell them you would like to study together. Be open to expanding your group with people you would not ordinarily be associated with.

Ask the school counselor for assistance in locating a study space. Outside of school, parents can assist. Faith-based groups may also provide space in a place that is safe and has restrooms and supervision. Once the group meetings commence, clearly define expectations for meaningful participation. Keep the team focused on its mission.

c) Practice self-tutoring by reading out loud.

When I really have to know something, it helps to claim it by reading it out loud. Getting ready to read aloud compels me to shut down the competing noises in my study area.

The private ritual of reading aloud is a reserved session for me and my senses only.

I tend to repeat important information aloud when I fail to get it right the first time. I don't give up till I pronounce words correctly. My voice fills the room. I am forced to hear it!

Joshy Washington says: "Also, when reading out loud, you are likely to catch dropped words, grammatical errors, and stilted, awkward word choices." This is absolutely true, especially when you read something you have written out loud.

The act of becoming engaged in the interactive ritual of reading aloud, allows you to participate in a self-tutoring session. You become your own best critic.

d) Seek the wisdom of caring elders.

If you don't have access to siblings or senior

members of your family with college degrees, you are at a disadvantage! Fix it. Take action to expand your networks to include wise, generous, caring adults who will assist you in your climb to the head of the class. Reach out and ask for a hand up, not a handout! Without these types of resources to support you in your educational journey, you will not likely do well in school or in life.

Daisaku Ikeda said: "Without a mentor in life, one can easily succumb to folly. Without a mentor in life, one can easily become self-centered, capricious and arrogant."

Social capital means to be rich in experience and have access to networks and social resources. Students from well-to-do backgrounds have many family and friends who have excelled. That comprises the social capital network that encourages them to stay the course. If you are the first in your family to compete and navigate in the unfamiliar sea of academic institutions, you will need to reach out to a coach or mentor.

GETTING IT RIGHT CASE STUDY

Individually, we are one drop. Together we are one ocean.

Ryunosuke Satoro

Jaime Escalante is a superstar in the history of urban education. He did what many thought was impossible. He taught high school students from poverty how to excel in college-level Advanced Placement (AP) Calculus. In 1982, 18 of his students from Garfield High School in East Los Angeles took and aced the AP Calculus test.

This outstanding feat by students from a historically low-performing school located in a disadvantaged district, with most of their parents lacking high school diplomas and fluency in English, was so improbable that a crisis ensued.

The staff of the most powerful testing and assessment organization in the world, the Educational Testing Service (ETS), suspected and accused the students of cheating. Jaime Escalante shot back at the finger pointers, claiming they were racists; however, he encouraged his students to re-take the test. They did so under the heightened scrutiny demanded by ETS. Once again, the students passed their AP Calculus exam with very impressive grades to boot.

The controversy and positive outcome for the underdogs grabbed headlines. The publicity caused a stir in educational circles around the country. Suddenly, there was a lot of interest in Jaime Escalante, his methods and students. Even the President of the United States took notice, so did the Governor of California.

Stories in the press began to appear about this

immigrant teacher from Bolivia who proved that students could be taught to earn the best grades in the most rigorous of math courses, no matter what their socio-economic status. This was huge.

The buzz among the students in the hallways, playground, cafeteria, library and gym at Garfield touted Jaime Escalante as the real deal. He was described as an inspirational teacher who motivated willing learners to master math. He became a magnet for those students who felt the desire to be more than what others had told them was possible. Gang bangers were not the only ones recruiting in East LA; the teacher from La Paz, Bolivia was there, too.

Escalante provided options to young Latinas and Latinos who otherwise might not have survived, let alone thrive in life. Their success made them realize that it was cool to excel in school. They began to take measurable steps for going places in the achievement universe where they had never gone before. He taught them how to take strides from simple math to algebra; to leap-frog from algebra to trigonometry; and to catapult from trig to AP Calculus.

The success of this remarkable immigrant educator and his students from the mean streets was captured in the movie, Stand and Deliver.

Edward James Olmos played the lead role in the film of Jaime Escalante and was nominated for a best actor Oscar for his work. This movie made famous the teacher who believed that students from poverty could excel, if they were thought to have ganas – a burning desire and focused determination to make it! The film has proven to be entertaining, instructive, and inspirational.

Jaime Escalante was fond of saying that it was "90 percent factual and 10 percent drama." Jerry Jesness, who is a special education teacher in Texas, interviewed and wrote about Escalante's critique of the film. In his article on the blog Reason.com, "Stand and Deliver Revisited..." he comments on the '10 percent' that Jaime said was not factual but drama instead:

Escalante tells me the film was 90 percent truth and 10 percent drama – but what a difference 10 percent can make. Stand and Deliver shows a group of poorly prepared, undisciplined young people who were initially struggling with fractions yet managed to move from basic math to calculus in just a year. The reality was far different.

It took 10 years to bring Escalante's program to peak success.

He didn't even teach his first calculus course until he had been at Garfield for several years. His basic math students from his early years were not the same students who later passed the AP Calculus test. (July, 2002, Issue).

The film, however, did not lie. It did its job. It was not released as a documentary. The drama components made it a successful film. It reached movie theaters as a piece of artistic entertainment to celebrate an important chapter in American education. Stand and Deliver is a metaphor of what Escalante, his students, their parents, community leaders and the educational team in his school accomplished over many years. The big plus of the film is that it celebrates a great teacher and students who went from being losers to becoming winners. The big minus is that it does not reveal how a mediocre student can become excellent or how an incompetent educator can become culturally competent and effective.

What did Jaime Escalante do in real life – factually – that was glossed over in the film? How did his former students describe his methods? How does his biographer explain his success at making his students excel in AP Calculus?

These sources explain that much happened in the ten years it took Jaime Escalante to build his program that produced the successful students in the film. Below are some of the strategies he implemented:

1. He cared and believed they could learn and they took steps to excel.

Mr. Escalante worked hard to win the minds and hearts of his students. He entertained them and employed dramatics to win their trust so as to become engaged in his classes. He uniquely employed all kinds of strategies to keep his students focused on their studies. Once they agreed to allow him to lead, he did it with gusto and more.

Esmeralda Bermudez from the Los Angeles Times wrote, "There was a time in East Los Angeles when el maestro's gruff voice bounced off his classroom walls. He roamed the aisles, he juggled oranges, he dressed in costumes, he punched the air, he called you names, he called your mom, he kicked you out, he lured you in, he danced, he boxed, he screamed, he whispered. He would do anything to get your attention. "(March 7, 2010).

Graciela Moreno, a reporter from KFSN-TV/DT, quotes Daniel Castro, a former student, now an attorney in North Fresno, who reflected on Escalante's life and legacy, and what he advocated: "A lot of the teachers and a lot of the administrators just didn't believe we could handle it, and Escalante changed that entire culture." He advocated: "…don't let someone believe in you more than you believe in yourself, and he believed in all of us." (April 1, 2010).

His students studied and graduated from high school and the best colleges and universities and made Escalante famous.

2. He persuaded them to stop wasting time and they followed his lead.

Escalante accused his students of being murderers. They killed time. They were lazy and unfocused. He had to shake them out of those ineffective habits, reports Matthews. The students were taught first to leverage their time before they could be taught to excel in their courses.

Claudio Sanchez, with National Public Radio (NPR), in his report, "Jaime Escalante's Legacy: Teaching Hope," revealed what the film glossed over:

"Fact is, Escalante's kids ate, slept and lived mathematics. They arrived an hour before school and stayed two, three hours after school. Escalante drilled them on Saturdays and made summer school mandatory. Some parents hated it, and they let Escalante know it." (March 30, 2010).

Another reporter from NPR documents how important it was for students to stay on task and to invest their "free time" from the classroom to continue to learn. Bates reports: "The Bolivian-born teacher believed math was the portal to any success his students could achieve later in life. So before school formally began, and after school ended, his door was open for extra help. And the students came on weekends and worked through holidays to prepare for the hardest exam of all – the Advanced Placement Calculus exam."

Delia Mora, one of his students, told Jay Mathews that Escalante worked so hard trying to teach them that the least they could do was work just as hard to learn. This meant not wasting precious time.

3. He made them tutors, which caused them to
    learn more by teaching others.

Students were encouraged to become tutors.
They were able to use more of their senses in the
process and thereby learned more of their math
by explaining it to others.

Karen Grisgby Bates, from NPR, writes in her
article, "Students 'Stand and Deliver' for Former
Teacher": "Escalante, whose students
mischievously nicknamed him 'Kimo' (a play on
The Lone Ranger's Kemosabe moniker), would
not only work with his students until they were all
ready to drop from exhaustion, he employed them
in the summers as tutors. And he showed them
that the best colleges in the country were not
beyond their reach." (March 9, 2010).

In the article by Bermudez in the LA Times,
Sergio Valdez, a former student of Escalante,
reflects on his beloved teacher and how
Escalante encouraged him to stop working in a
liquor store and tutor instead: "Everything I've
done I owe to him." Today, Valdez works at the
Jet Propulsion Laboratory. "He carries with him
the belief that he can accomplish anything,"
reports Bermudez.

4. He advocated for his students and they
    protected him in return.

Escalante put his professional life on the line for
his students. He created rules that did not bode
well with high school administrators. For example,

he insisted that his students come to class prepared and ready to learn, having done their homework, ready for productive discussion. Before they could enter his classroom, they had to answer a homework question.

Jesness explains how that went over: "He had already earned the criticism of an administrator, who disapproved of his requiring the students to answer a homework question before being allowed into the classroom."

The film documents how his students protected his property from vandalism and how they painted his car. In 2010, when cancer struck and Mr. Escalante was nearing the end of his life, having depleted his funds on medical interventions, former students, community residents and parents joined actor Olmos for a Garfield fundraiser.

Bates quotes another former student: "Everything we are, we owe to him," said Sandra Munoz. She revealed how Escalante tapped her on the shoulder and invited her to join his advance math class:

"He'd see someone and decide they needed to be in his class. So he pulled me out of my sophomore year and put me in his class, and I took math with him. He would teach anybody who wanted to learn – they didn't have to be designated gifted and talented by the school." Today, Sandra is an attorney who advocates for the rights of workers and immigrants in East LA.

5. He urged them to study in small groups to multiply learning and they did.

Jay Mathews, in his book Escalante: The Best Teacher in America documented how trying to find a place to study on weekends became a challenge. Schools were closed then. While students who had parents with means had rooms with desks, books and parents to discuss problems with, or could buy a seat in a Sylvan or Huntington learning and/or tutoring for pay facility, Garfield High School students could not afford those venues, and their living spaces were too small.

So, they went to a local fast food chain restaurant for breakfast on Saturday mornings to study, in small groups, with their favorite teacher. Escalante treated them to their tasty hot meal.

The manager of the restaurant eventually told them that they were not welcome. The students made their breakfast purchases and they used the facility to study, making it impossible for other customers to find seats for their meals. The teacher and his students were in a constant struggle to shut out the noise and find conducive areas for study and productive small group discussions. Community homework centers were in short supply in East LA, but that didn't stop them. They were on a mission.

6. He had as much ganas to teach as they developed to learn.

The teacher made a partnership with his students. He would work hard, and they would too. Parents from well-to-do backgrounds spend countless hours facilitating the learning process. They work hard with their children to do well in school. But what if parents from the Barrios or the hood don't know how to do that? They need teachers who will put ownership on those students as though they were their guardians.

In essence, they need to become parental figures. At least, that's what Escalante demonstrated had to happen at Garfield High. To Jaime, teaching was not just a job, it was a vocation.

Escalante had as much ganas to teach as his students developed to learn. He knew that without providing tutoring and getting the students in his class to bond and study in small groups, they might fail. So they studied into the night inside the school. He was their after-school adult connection.

Students shared with NPR reporter Bates what that meant: "Escalante tutored his students until late at night, piled them into his minivan and brought them home to their parents, who trusted Escalante in ways they never would other teachers…" Aríceli Lerma remembers: "My mother used to stay up, not to check up on him, but to bring him a plate of food because she knew how hard he was working!"

7. He engaged parents, teachers, the counselor and his principal to boost their grades.

Escalante could not have done it alone. A whole team effort is responsible for his celebrated success.

Reports his biographer: "All students who joined the calculus team, or its underclass farm clubs, would have to sign, along with their parents, a paper promising attention, homework, good attendance, and consistent effort in all their classes. He would in turn promise to teach them what they needed to know."

If the parents were not engaged, progress was impossible. The students needed to promise excellence in other classes. Together they created the teaching/learning platform.

His principal was also there, creating the space for Jaime to work with his students. Jaime once got in trouble with a school official who wanted him fired for inconveniencing the janitor of the high school. The janitor complained that Escalante was coming too early to school and staying too late, in order to help his students. An assistant principal threatened to have him fired. Jesness and others have documented how his new principal, Henry Gradillas, supported Escalante and gave him a set of keys to the school. The problem was solved. The visionary principal allowed Escalante to have control of his program.

There was a need for flexibility on how traditional resources could be used for helping students before and after regular class sessions.

Gradillas gave Escalante whatever he needed to facilitate his best work. Writes Mathews: "As far as Gradillas was concerned… Escalante… had passed all the important tests. He was loyal to the school. He stayed in touch with his principal. He loved the kids. He taught with a passion that filled Gradillas with wonder. By 1983 the principal was asking Escalante for a list of his needs. 'Whatever you need, I'll get. You have Carta Blanca.' Escalante said he wanted more books, a teaching assistant, and a new room." The principal made it happen.

Mathews also documented how Jaime engaged counselor Ed Martin in helping students he sent to the office for not doing their homework to advocate on the students' behalves and beg Escalante to take them back. The students would have to promise the counselor that if he could get Escalante to take them back, they would always do their homework. Students agreed and so did Escalante. This strategy worked. Without the counselor's collaboration, Escalante would not have succeeded.

There were teachers who worked side by side with him. Mr. Ben Jimenez got outstanding results from his AP courses.

He also secured cooperation from the parents who had signed contracts with Escalante allowing their children to study instead of doing chores that competed with his rigorous efforts.

Jay Mathews reports that Escalante once admonished one of his students, who stopped by to thank him because, as she explained: "We are learning." He said to her: "One day you are going to be using math, and if you are using math, remember you learned it over here. But don't remember me, remember Garfield. You have to remember the school, and remember that math is fun. And, that you were part of the team."

It took a whole community to educate Garfield students to excel in complex math. The film celebrates only one major force - Jaime Escalante.

I encourage you to watch the film Stand and Deliver more than once. But don't fall into the trap of believing that the story of Escalante and the students as related in the film can be used as a roadmap to success. There is no way for students lacking the basic math skills at the beginning of the school year to master AP Calculus by its conclusion. It does not work that way.

To climb to the head of the class, you have to read what his former students said he urged them to do, what his biographer revealed and what this chapter proposes. Each of these components reinforces the other. Doing just one thing, like finding a caring teacher, is a great beginning, but not enough. What the film did not fully capture, you must not ignore in your quest to be the best.

Las ganas to persevere together with a holistic plan is what will get you to the head of the class.

CONCLUSION

It takes all of your senses to educate a whole brain. Dr. William Osler, one of the most celebrated physicians in history, said, "Observe, read, tabulate, and communicate. Use your five senses, learn to see, hear, learn to feel, learn to smell, and know that by practice you can become expert."

To excel in your school work, you must also study with like-minded peers who are the real deal - no teamwork, no success. That's why you need to join or create study groups.

Jaime Escalante was a great educator. He dedicated his life to helping students survive through education. He is one of many. President Obama said, "Jaime's story became famous. But he represented countless, valiant teachers throughout our country whose great works are known only to the young people whose lives they change."

Never forget that there are also adults in every profession, like Escalante, who have the social capital and who, if asked, would be willing to become your coach or mentor. Get out of your comfort zone and ask.

Then, you have a reciprocal obligation to help

others. That is a great way to learn. Small group discussions multiply learning. So don't study solo. Not now, not ever. It's your turn to leverage your senses, to network, to graduate, and most important to stand and deliver.

STEP 7

Stop Viewing Educators as Mean Abusive Adults

Throughout life people will make you mad,
disrespect you and treat you bad.
Let God deal with the things they do, 'cause
hate in your heart will consume you, too.

Will Smith

WHY YOU MUST GET IT RIGHT!

Adultists exist. Believe me, I know. Please don't confuse the word adultist with adultery, which refers to marital infidelity. Adultism is a different word. It has to do with adults who treat their subordinates in an unfair, demeaning and often insulting manner. Adultists believe that because they are older, it is acceptable behavior to bully those who are younger and for whom they are 'responsible.'

Adultists give authority figures a bad name. They create hostility across generations. Victims who experience this at home tend to develop issues with authority figures throughout their lives. They are more prone to question or defy the authority of adults with legitimate power.

Genuine educators, who hold the key to success, are mistakenly put into this category of adultists. Sadly, those targeted by adultism fail to differentiate between abusive and supportive adults.

Protecting yourself from abusive adults begins with understanding the logic – however faulty - that causes them to justify being adultists. Figuring out how to excel in school in spite of the antagonistic environment at home is another.

My relationships with caring adults, competent educators, and generous authors of memoirs filled with hopeful stories and role models, and a reformed grandfather, allowed me to bounce back from adversity and complete my studies. I became an educator. Eventually, I started my own family, free from toxic adultism, where love and respect flows across generations.

Age-Driven Belligerence by Adults Against Youth at Home

Dealing with adultism became a huge challenge for me when I was young. It was terrible. You may have the similar misfortune of dealing with adultists in your life.

When confronting this type of age-driven belligerence, some young people resist through passive/aggressive behavior. They drag their feet when expected to be quick. They fume and protest while doing their chores. Some will text their friends, complaining about their parents. Excellence seldom defines their completed tasks. They also become very adept at disappearing from the radar of the adultists in their lives. Phone calls and text messages from parents are ignored. Some youth even put their safety at risk by becoming confrontational with their more powerful, unreasonable and intimidating elders.

We grow up thinking that adults in positions of authority are bound to be like our parents. This can be both good and bad.

If you are shaped by loving parents, who discipline but do not punish and who are guided by a sense of fairness, you will likely look upon adults as worthy of admiration and trust; not as adultists. The reverse is also true. If your parents behave boorishly, are impolite and rough, then they will likely poison your view of older people and you will grow up thinking that adults are uncaring, selfish and unworthy of respect.

When your parents behave like adultists, you tend to adopt a love/hate relationship with them. If you cannot talk back for fear of being slapped or losing privileges, you mutter counter hostilities under your breath and may even do deviant things to protest your victimization. Worse, you may also have older siblings following in your parents' dreadful footsteps, being pushy and disrespectful of your dignity. If you have younger siblings, you may be behaving like an adultist by pushing them around.

I once heard a parent say, "Children become what we are, not what we tell them to be." If that is true, and you live with adultists, keep reading and learning why that must not become characteristic of your behavior in adulthood.

See if you recognize this scene. Your father or mother comes home, walks into the TV room and, without any concern for what you or others may be watching, simply changes the channel to whatever program suits his or her fancy. You have just been ignored. Your self-worth has just been diminished. You feel humiliated. You are burning up inside, but helpless to do anything about it. It really hurts, especially when these insensitive figures happen to be your parents. It does not help that you depend on them for food, shelter, clothing and much more.

Adultists will interrupt your conversation with friends to send you on errands. They will remain unaware and/or unconcerned about the importance of what you were doing. They can just as easily interrupt a school-networking meeting, a delicate matter of the heart or a gathering with peers to socialize. Whatever you are doing has to stop, and quickly. There are some adultists who believe that you are not completing the tasks with enough speed and do not hesitate to get physical with you, even in front of your peers. Ouch! That really hurts. There is no room for objection. You must simply obey. In the adultist mind, children have no rights that adults need to respect.

They truly believe this atrocious and overbearing behavior is justified.

Adultists demand absolute obedience on command. They rationalize this demand by firmly believing young ones under their care are learning responsibility. The same rubbish they were fed is what they now serve to the next generation. They may go so far as to believe their harshness builds character and good work habits in their children.

They may be busy doing serious things on the computer, loafing around, reading magazines, watching TV or glued to their cell phones when suddenly, the land-line phone rings. They yell, "Answer the phone!" At other times:

- "See who is at the door."

- "Get me a drink!"

- "Take out the garbage!"

- "Get out of my sight!"

- "Which part of right now don't you understand?"

- "Turn down that music."

- "Get those plugs out of your ears."

- "Set the table."

- "Clean your room."

- "Turn off the computer."

- "Are you listening to me?"

- "Go to the store and get a gallon of milk."

- "Take the dog for a walk."

Don't get me wrong. Parents have a right to expect that you contribute to the collective good of the family by doing errands. Asking you to do things to lessen their burden is not wrong. It is not in the asking, but in the way they ask that determines rudeness. When parents shout commands in an urgent and menacing tone of voice, the task they want you to complete becomes very unappealing. The threat of violence and other negative consequences must never be the reason why good things must be done. The absence of loving incentives in the 'requests' generates seething anger on the part of younger members of the family. Adultists can suffocate your inner-self. They tell you what to do in a shabby manner so often that you conclude you just won't do anything. You may even be tempted to give up believing in yourself.

Youth Acting Out Against Adult Educators in School

As a pushed, punished and pummeled victim, you arrive at school prepared to reject adultist behavior. You act out, resulting in trouble with teachers, peers, principals and counselors; above all, yourself. Students beware. Do not practice "reverse ageism."

Age does not make enemies of all adults. Reject adultism, not adults! In your efforts to protect yourself from what is clearly abusive and destructive, you may also be rejecting forces that are essential, affirming and constructive in your quest to the head of the class. When you shut out caring teachers, you are closing the door to academic success and the eventual independence from the real adultists in your life. Educators can listen as you vent and, when asked; they can help you explore ways to protect yourself from being victimized. Caring, sensitive adults who want you to excel in school can be your best resource for getting out of harm's way.

If you are a product of an adultist upbringing and want to succeed in school, stop and think about the forces that might propel you toward academic failure. You may confuse directives to accomplish tasks by a positive, forceful teacher as crass disregard for your dignity, humanity and freedom. In your eyes, such teachers must be resisted. When you enter school ready to defy anyone representing authority, you may wind up shooting yourself in the foot. You need to be conscious of the types of defiant behaviors that constitute the ineffective habit of viewing educators as adultists.

Acts of defiance do not have to be vicious, full of

rage, or explosive in nature to have a deadly impact. Students become very sophisticated at learning how to push the right buttons aimed at getting teachers upset without crossing the line, which can earn them a quick trip to the principal's office or a suspension. It starts when a student withdraws their sense of respect for adults as educators.

Negative Impact of Acting Out

A disrespectful spirit encourages further acts of defiance, making schools places of resentment and conflict. Students become indifferent to class assignments. Walking into the classroom is done with calculated lethargy.

Finding a seat takes forever. Slamming books on desks and sitting with an "I don't care" attitude follows. They neither sit at attention, nor express eagerness to become engaged in the dialogue that guides the process of learning. These students reject the serious purposes of teaching and learning with every fiber of their being.

Defiant students talk when they should be listening and remain silent when invited to express their ideas. At times, they write obscenities in their textbooks. They are absorbed in texting rather than listening. They raise their hands for permission to go to the bathroom more often than to contribute in the classroom. They fuel the energy of other students who act like bullies or fools. They pester or try to intimidate serious students.

In numerous ways, these students terrorize the classroom and poison the peaceful climate for a healthy learning experience. Sometimes sexual or racial harassment becomes part of the defiance. As a result, no predictable progress to the head of the class is possible. In their quest to get even with adultists, they cheat themselves and throw obstacles at others in the classroom, making it even more difficult for everyone to succeed.

Troublemakers in the classroom are often so successful at creating chaos, thwarting both teaching and learning, that they cause new teachers entering the profession to abandon their ideals or desire to teach where needs are greatest. Teachers emotionally rejected by students withdraw respect and affection in return.

Once the classroom is transformed into a war zone, learning becomes the greatest casualty. When enough bad experiences frighten teachers into reacting harshly to get their turf back, don't be surprised if you wind up with an adultist, even if you did not start out with one. It is important not to perceive your teachers as abusive dictatorial forces who should be shunned, confronted, sabotaged or disobeyed. This will result in losing the support, wise counsel, educational guidance, coaching and instructional input for successfully graduating and becoming free of adultist relationships. Please don't fall into that trap. You

must learn to identify supportive adults, follow
their lead, and seek their advice on how to deal
with a hostile environment at home.

STRATEGIES FOR SUCCESS

When you hold resentment toward another, you
are bound to that person or condition by an
emotional link that is stronger than steel.
Forgiveness is the only way to dissolve that link
and get free.

Catherine Ponder

a) Choose collaboration instead of confrontation with caring adults.

If you are a respectful, considerate and
productive student who follows the lead of caring
adults, keep up the good work! You are a true
blessing. This is especially true if you have had
adultists in your life tempting you to distrust other
authority figures. You must continue to show
respect for those in positions of authority,
especially educators. The abusive behaviors that
have robbed you of your past cannot be allowed
to fester and rob you of your future.

The good news is there are teachers who,
contrary to adultist scripts, seek nothing more
than to help guide you into becoming your best
self. The cruel adultist game that may have been

inflicted on you must not serve as a motivational factor for you to inflict pain on yourself.

Don't hurt yourself – excel! The best revenge is success. Dig deep into your inner being. Find in that core what you want to become and pursue those desires. An education is indispensable for that purpose. Continue to choose collaboration instead of confrontation.

b) Don't become the anti-hero in school.

If you are a problem student in school – stop. Being an anti-hero, pushing buttons to sabotage the teaching/learning agenda and displaying disrespectful body language in front of teachers creates havoc in the classroom. In the process, you may become heroic in the eyes of a few who applaud your antics. However, when the laughter dies down, everybody loses. You stand to lose the most. Teachers talk to each other and you will develop a reputation. In becoming a problem to others, you cheat yourself of their guidance and sabotage your own growth.

This downward spiral toward self-destruction must be stopped. You must give teachers the opportunity to demonstrate that they care and are worthy of respect. In some cases, you may find educators who exhibit adultist behavior, but you should not label all teachers as abusive adults. To assume that all teachers behave as adultists is foolhardy and unfair.

The truth is that many educators want their

students to succeed more than students themselves want to excel. You must expect that teachers will help and guide you, rather than hinder your goal for learning and graduating. Give respectful collaboration a chance. Don't play the fool in school. In the end, you lose.

c) **Seek counseling from caring respectful educators.**

The more educational progress you make, the more your hopes for getting out of an adultist relationship will be actualized. Get rid of the habit of viewing all teachers as adultists. If you get rid of this ineffective habit, you might be pleasantly surprised to find a pool of talented professionals who are passionate about their subject matter and totally respectful of your dignity, self-worth and quest for empowerment.

You must always express gratitude to those who seek to guide you through a better way of doing something. Do what they require to widen your horizons and universalize your spirit. Expect teachers to teach you and counselors to counsel you. Meet their highest expectations in return. Receive direction, complete your homework and succeed.

Indignities experienced at the hands of adultists may clutter your path to learning and maturity. The wisdom of generous educators must be tapped to help remove obstacles. Talk to your peers and see if they know the educators who are the "real deal." Seek out the educator with a reputation for having a listening ear and let him or her know that you need to chat privately. Explain your situation at home. Express your desire to do well in life and in school. Ask for a series of strategies you can implement to deal with the adultist reality at home. They might suggest that you start simply; get up and make your bed, throw out the garbage, limit watching TV or talking on your cell phone. Then you can focus more on behaving in school and maybe doing other chores without being told; these voluntary acts will help prevent adultists from yelling orders and making you feel miserable.

d) Read to protect yourself from adultists and learn how not to become one.

Professionals who have dedicated their lives to the healing process of abuse victims have also published books and articles about difficult parents, teachers and bullies.

If you learn to listen to the words of wisdom in the literature, you too will be able to find courage and inspiration to excel in life.

Read and heed the wise counsel of experts who have written about adultism. For example, Understanding Adultism: a Key to Developing Positive Youth – Adult Relationships by John Bell; and, Discrimination against Youth Voice by Adam Fletcher offer valuable insights.

Books such as Toxic Parents: Overcoming their Hurtful Legacy and Reclaiming Your Life by Dr.

Susan Howard; Surviving a Borderline Parent by
Kimberlee Roth and Freda B. Friedman; or, the
memoir of a young person's struggle and victory
over an abusive childhood by Bryan Nash,
entitled: A Phoenix Rising: Defining the Moments;
a True Story of Triumph over Child Abuse, are
worth reading.

GETTING IT RIGHT CASE STUDY

Hanging on to resentment is letting someone you
despise live rent free in your head.

Ann Landers

Let me share with you my own encounter with
adultist behavior. What I am going to reveal is not
pretty. My grandfather was the first adultist in my
life. When my mom was a little girl, he would
punch her in the face and one night after a
thrashing, he even locked her up in a filthy, dark,
smelly latrine as punishment. My mother wanted
to get out of her traditional woman's role in rural
Puerto Rico in the 1930s. She wanted to get an
education and become a teacher. Her hopes and
dreams were violently resisted by her parents.

My grandfather held deep resentment for my
mother's refusal to stay and help take care of her
younger siblings. Matters got worse when she
took an additional step of disobedience: she
eloped and left the island with a man he intensely

disliked. When the marriage failed while living in New York, she decided to take my brothers and I back to her native Puerto Rico. My father remained in the States. He was more than willing to pay for our one-way airfares to the island rather than having to pay continuous child support in New York.

Once we arrived in Puerto Rico, she left the three of us at her parents' house. My mom went to another town to work as a maid in the home of a wealthy family.

She planned to make enough money to return to New York and then she would send for us. So now, as a single mom with a bunch of kids, she returned home to seek help from her parents.

My grandfather saw us as a curse. He decided to take out his anger on us because he could not punish his daughter. We could stay, but we had to pay for our upkeep by working as hired hands in the hacienda (plantation) that he supervised. We were innocent children, but that did not matter. He pushed us to take manly responsibilities at the tender ages of seven, eight, and eleven years old. When we failed to meet his unrealistic expectations, he took it as a personal insult and act of insubordination. Verbal attacks led to intense physical abuse.

My grandfather took better care of his domestic animals than his grandkids. He saw the farm animals as valuable resources, but his grandkids were an albatross around his neck. He had six children of his own. He did not need my mother bringing him three more. He was furious that his daughter had not taken steps to lessen his load as the culture expected and he demanded. In his eyes, she made his life worse.

My brothers and I were caught in the middle of their conflict. As little kids, we began our fragile journey through life at the mercy of a very angry and powerful adultist. We were never allowed to sit at the dinner table and eat with him.

He would shout and rant with angry outbursts for us to be quiet. When he walked into a room, we would shudder with fear. There was no tenderness in him. He would keep a list of our infractions and save them. That way, a future punishment session for one infraction could include cashing in for the others.

He once held the wrists of my two brothers with a vice-like grip, while viciously beating them with a rope – the hot scalding tears, desperate cries for mercy and frantic, hysterical pulls toward freedom did not compel him to stop. Only when he was exhausted did the beating stop. By then my brothers had soiled themselves and fainted. We lived in constant fear of having to pay what was owed. We sometimes wet the bed, which became another reason to get spankings from my aunts, who followed his lead as sources of abuse.

My mother came to visit us. When she listened to our complaints, she was appalled. She took us out of his house and gave us away to strangers!

She shopped around for residents in the valley who needed errand boys to work for room and board. We were dispersed and soon became errand-running gofers for adults without affinity toward us. We learned to live lives devoid of affection. I don't remember ever being told as a child, "I am so proud of you," or "that a' boy."

We were sent to fetch water from distant streams and gather kindling wood in 'la finca' deep inside the land. We delivered bottles of milk and returned with fresh eggs from isolated neighbors. Our duties included taking food to the man of the house in the midst of a gang of workers during the harvest. In order to go to school, we had to walk for long distances.

On the other side of the emotional pendulum, not only did we lack protection from those who were supposed to love us, but we became targets and victims of sexual predators as innocent little boys.

It took 68 years before my oldest living brother had a birthday celebrated in his honor. My wife and I hosted the event when he finally connected with us after his sojourn as a loner and a recovering addict. I noticed his eyes were moist and he had a lump in his throat. I took him aside and asked why. He said that this birthday party constituted the first time that anything had been celebrated in his honor – ever! He did not weep alone.

Our lives took twists and turns from those early days of anguish, tears and separation. My brother, who is one year older, worked with a family that kept him out of school and had him brew illegal booze instead. The other worked tending domestic animals for another family. I was farmed out to the house of the public works man – he was 'el caminero' - the keeper of the road.

In the wee hours of the morning, he drank strong, fresh, hot black coffee and was off. He often worked a long distance from home, patching up roads with tar and keeping the gutters by the side of roads clean. Mudslides from the hills after heavy rains required him to remove obstructions on a continuous basis. Drivers going from one town to another would alert him of the work that needed to be done.

It would be my responsibility to take him a hot breakfast around 9 a.m. Later, I would do the same with his lunch around half past noon.

Their daughter was younger than I was. She became jealous and mean to me, but they didn't do anything to stop her. I slept in a corner on the wooden floor. I felt very alone in that house. In one of my errands to take food to 'el caminero,' I found out how to get to my grandparents' house, so I decided to run away.

I took my meager belongings, put them in a paper bag, took my 'mocho' - a very old, overused, rusted machete - and off I went to my grandparents. I cried and begged them to take me back. My grandmother took pity on me. She tried to convince my grandfather to allow me to stay. I was frail and seemingly the most helpless of the bunch. He finally agreed. Working there became more tolerable for me.

Not long after that, my older brother also sought refuge with our grandparents. When my grandfather saw him at a distance, he became outraged. He chased him and threw rocks at him. When he eventually caught him, he held my brother by the back of the neck, took him to the main road and waited for the big bus to come. Once a day, 'la guagua grande' - the big bus, would travel across the mountain barrios, picking up passengers on its way to the major port city in the region.

He signaled the bus to stop, took his grandson up the steps and found a window seat for him. He then paid the driver a one-way fare to take the little boy to the end of the line. No further instructions were given to the driver or to my brother. That was that. He got rid of his problem.

My brother was nine years old. I have no idea what thoughts were stirring in his head as that bus snaked its way down the long, narrow, winding roads through the tropical, mountain, coffee region of Puerto Rico on its way to a big coastal city he had never been to. Adrift, wounded, penniless and alone, he would have to figure it out.

My grandfather was the first person I ever hated…

My mother managed to return to the US and send for us. Years later, as a young adult, I decided to return to Mayaguez, Puerto Rico. The Civil Rights Movement inspired me to learn more about my roots. I wanted to sharpen my Spanish speaking skills and deepen my cultural understanding of my island heritage. I also wanted to learn more about the race issue, Puerto Rican style.

In my quest to become a competent professional, I found myself studying at a college not far from where I had spent my childhood. I did not intend to visit my grandfather; however, our paths would inevitably cross.

One afternoon while I was working on a research paper on race relations, there was a knock on my dormitory door.

I opened it and was flabbergasted. It was my grandfather. The dean of students brought him to my residence. He was much older, shorter and humbler than I remembered him. He was not the tall dictator who had ruled the plantation from his mighty horse, machete by his side, barking orders to the hundreds of peasant workers during the coffee harvest season. He was no longer the man who struck fear in the hearts of his grandchildren. He appeared to be very human, with a vulnerability and warmth that drew me to him. However, a flood of painful memories quickly clouded my vision.

My grandfather looked me in the eye, removed his dressy boater type straw hat with the white band around the crown, held it to his chest and uttered the words, "Forgive me, my son... Forgive me."

It was an emotional stick-up! I was disarmed by this display of affection. I went through a cultural shift as he opened his arms to me and confessed that he had treated me harshly. I was overcome with conflicting emotions; however, we embraced and cried together. He felt so human, warm and loving, like a grandparent is supposed to feel. For the first time, I experienced the power of his love.

As I write this, I realize that this was the first time I had received a hug from a father figure. I was 22 years old!

The tears and profound deep sobbing ritual, which framed that defining moment, washed away the bitterness I harbored. We began to grow in love and appreciate each other. He was amazed by my educational journey and my sophistication as a young man. I was in my junior year of college and becoming fluent in both Spanish and English. In turn, I found him to be a spiritual person who had learned through religious conversion to become compassionate, humble, patient and generous. He had gotten rid of the jagged edges. He was a new man. The adultist hurtful behaviors that once defined him had been replaced by his new passion as a minister of the Gospel. His new mission was to bring people together instead of tearing them apart. Who would have thought this transformation was possible?

On that sunny tropical afternoon with a gentle breeze under the flame trees on top of a hill overlooking the coastal city of Mayagüez, our intense, honest communication about new beginnings allowed our humanity to flow like a sweet transfusion into each other's spirit. The healing journey had begun in earnest. We agreed to stay in contact with each other. We did.

Our love for each other flourished during the sunset years of his life. By the time he died at age 93, he had become my beloved 'abuelito' - grandpa – no longer the tyrant who had terrorized the spirit of my childhood. I lived to see him hug and kiss his three great grandchildren, my children, whom I brought for a visit to enrich his life. Before leaving his house in the town of Aguada, on our journey back to San Juan, he would pick fruit and cut sugar cane for us. We would make a circle and hold hands. He would pray loudly and fervently over us. He would again shower us with hugs and kisses. We always took pictures near the big colorful 'amapola', the-hibiscus flowers in the garden near his house. Cristina, David and Daniel were not much older than my brothers and I when his adultist spirit ruled. It was surreal.

My one regret is that he was never able to make peace with my brothers. They would never again trust adults as authority figures in their lives. They were problem children and graduated into troubled adults. My older brother, who my mom kept while we were given away, became a gang leader, went to prison and died violently.

The second became a chronic alcoholic and the third a functional alcoholic. Illegal drugs created havoc in the fabric of their beings. It's ironic that, in so many ways, for many years, they beat themselves up with greater destructiveness than the adultists in their lives ever did.

Now, one of them lectures and provides wise counsel to recovering addicts on how to make sense of their lives. He accompanies me when I lecture in the Chicago area. I am very proud of him. The other one has a gift for making other people laugh. He loves football games on TV and watching re-runs of Seinfeld. He enjoys the company of his wife and daughter in Chicago and communicates often with his older daughter in London. On occasion, we play dominoes.

The three of us also visit Puerto Rico once a year, trying to create good memories before our final farewells. At times, we have driven through the mountain region of our childhood in silence. We are growing closer to each other, but it has not been easy.

You may not be experiencing the type of cruelty I have described. Nevertheless, you may be a victim of incompetent parents. There may be adults in your life who make you miserable.

Get educated on your road to building a healthy relationship with yourself and acquire the skills to assist adultist relatives to transform into compassionate family members. Embrace the rewards of forgiving.

Desmond Tutu from South Africa wisely reminds us that "Without forgiveness, there's no future."

CONCLUSION

Growing up in the home of incompetent parents and guardians is painful at times, to say the least. Adultism constitutes bullying younger people with commands, threats, and punishment to do the bidding of elders. If you are in that kind of situation, you run the risk not only of turning against mean-spirited adults but also against caring, sensitive ones. Be careful. Don't reject adults in the name of rejecting adultism. Become pro-active in doing your chores and becoming a useful member of your family networks. When you get busy doing what needs to be done, you won't have to be bullied into being 'responsible'.

I was lucky to make peace with my formerly adultist grandfather. Be ready to forgive should the opportunity come your way. In the meantime, if that is not possible, having an education allows you to eventually get out of harm's way. Read and learn how to cope from the memoirs of people who thrived in spite of abusive rearing. Choose educated friends who are generous and full of life. Never forget that the best revenge is success. Meanwhile, if you are fortunate to have loving, sensitive parents, honor them with your academic success.

STEP 8

Stop Yielding to Tech-Driven Distractions

These days, the number of technologically-advanced and tempting ways that students can ignore their academic obligations has skyrocketed!

Naomi Rockler-Gladen

WHY YOU MUST GET IT RIGHT!

Students beware! Spending too much time online will inevitably cause irreparable harm to your academic careers! Don't 'click' your life away. It's not worth it. Use technology, don't let it use you. Think of it as essentially good, but potentially dangerous.

The three forces that will seduce you into yielding to tech-related distractions, at the expense of your academic success, can be likened to the convergence of three distinct forces in nature to create a weather phenomenon that Sebastian Junger popularized in his book, The Perfect Storm.

A metaphorical adaptation of the forces shaping

the 'perfect storm' describes how high-tech resources simultaneously interacting with three negative behaviors can derail and destroy your quest to excel:

- The warm weather flowing from a low-pressure system could represent your becoming lazy, bored and vulnerable to high-tech attractions. These gadgets hurl you into a whirlwind of fun, electrifying and time-consuming activities, which wipe out your will, wits and wisdom for figuring out how to climb to the head of the class.

- The flow of cool and dry air generated by a high pressure system could represent the computer and the sleek networks of high-tech gadgets. They blow your carelessly cruising mindset toward immediate gratification and time-killing destinations, thereby, uprooting, spinning and trashing your educational plans.

- The tropical moisture in the form of a hurricane could be generated by your curiosity-driven compulsion for 'sexting' and visiting porn websites that enrage your hormones with sexually explicit images and products that provoke lust, enticement and overexcitement. Thereby, deviating, corrupting and exhausting the creative energies needed for completing your school assignments.

These types of high-tech distractions constitute a real and pressing danger for every student who wants to excel. They can pull you down to failure or push you up to success. The choice is yours. If they seduce you, they are likely to strangle your serious purposes. Therefore, you must think critically about where you want technology resources to take you.

It is important to note that technology is not the villain in this perfect storm. It is the more elusive lack of discipline that fills this role. As 21st century students, you will need a steady, disciplined use of high-tech resources to achieve your best hopes. Just don't get sidetracked by time-wasting activities.

Before I fall into the trap of stereotyping, let me congratulate the many of you who have steered clear from becoming bored and vulnerable to tech distractions. Your involvements keep you hard at work, focused on your studies and dedicated to helping others. Your passion for living with a commitment to being productive and doing your fair share deserves to be recognized.

You too may be outraged by the morally loose, corner-cutting lifestyle of freeloaders who do not see that using high-tech resources for enrichment and improving the quality of life is the smart way to go.

In this chapter, I will focus on high-tech related distractions and how to keep them from having a negative impact on your studies.

Benefits and Value of Technology

The benefits and added value of technology in my life are many. The fun stuff that frames my life depends on the blessings of high-tech platforms. Receiving and sending photos of loved ones via email and multimedia messages (MMS) on my cell phone is the best. Watching a great epic film or an old Western on HDTV with my wife, or viewing an animated film with the grandkids adds serenity to our lives. High-tech venues add value to these priceless moments.

I travel a great deal. Flying is made so much more bearable and comfortable when I take my iPod.

I purchased luxury earplugs to connect to the eclectic options of songs and entertainers that keep me company during long hours on flights. I also recently downloaded Skype onto my computer. This allows me to have face-to-face conversations via webcam with family, friends and members of my mentoring network at no additional cost to my Internet bill. Business is made easier with cutting-edge communication technology; virtual operations have become indispensable for my work team, my associates and me.

Technology is an invaluable time saver. Instead of spending hours in front of the TV, gathering news and information from various channels, I can turn on my computer and obtain news stories immediately. This shaves hours off of keeping up with what is going on in the country and the world.

A great deal of my work also requires research. Internet resources have helped me obtain relevant information in minutes, which, without technology, may have taken me hours or even days to find. For example, 80 percent of the information I have obtained for this book was done with the help of technology. However, without activating your 'distraction detectors', you might get sucked into the whirlwind of never-ending allurements that are made readily available through technology.

What Is a 'Distraction Detector?'

A distraction detector is an internal defense mechanism in your psyche that propels you to take evasive action in the face of high-tech threats. It works like the invisible shield that protected the Endor moon in Star Wars.

A developed mindset keeps you from getting into trouble. It works like the small blinking red light by the gas gauge on the dashboard - sometimes referred to as the 'idiot light.' The blinking light serves as a wakeup call to the driver to stop being distracted and get to the gas pump.

The distraction detector mindset plays a similar role in transmitting warning signals about the pitfalls of entering the super high-tech highway of time-absorbing activities.

"If you do," the internal device warns, "you are going to run out of 'fuel'," - the time and creative energies needed to complete your school projects. Think of a distraction detector, then, as a small red light on the dashboard of your conscience, blinking warnings when you need to practice self-control.

Early warning signals must not be ignored. If you do, it will cost you the peace of mind, precision and focus needed to excel in your school projects. When the perfect storm heads your way, you will need the fuel to flee from its destructive path. Distraction detectors provide warnings so you do not get caught in the storm.

Think of the distraction detector as a series of automatic gut-to-brain responses, which keep you from potentially harmful situations. When we were small children, our parents told us not to accept candy, gifts, or rides from strangers. They warned us not to walk through dark alleys. However, the best protection device they cultivated, as we got older, was our own ability to detect and flee from perceived threats.

The ability to recognize such dangers keeps us safer! For example, built-in cues and reinforcements, like looking both ways when crossing the street or traveling in groups, as well as calling home when we reach our destinations, has provided us with protective shields. It is because we activate these shields that we remain safe and enjoy life.

Remember, those tips were not meant to keep us from enjoying family and friends, or to keep us from becoming part of social groups or visiting others. They were put there to keep us from potential harm.

The pep talks from our families helped us stay away from danger, being manipulated, or experiencing troubled encounters or abuse from authority figures. Those caution triggers in our brains, put there by our parents, will stay with us forever. You have them in your mind. I still have them in mine.

Human beings can be your friends, teachers, mentors - sources of love and inspiration - or they can be a source of danger. Technology is the same. You need to know when to embrace it and when to flee from it.

Only you can activate your distraction detectors and say no to high-tech driven distractions lurking in your path to excel. Why? Since you probably know more about the complex world of technology than your parents, it becomes your responsibility to inform your mindset and activate the safeguards.

Even while appearing to be in front of the computer studying, you are likely to be bombarded with temptations to abandon your studies. The biggest distractions come from your network of peers, friends and loved ones in the form of phone calls, text messages, emails, and postings on social websites. Before you know it, your creative energies are spent and your tasks remain undone.

Every time you pleasure-seek through the computer, answer the cell phone, engage in a texting exchange, plug your ears with music, play videos, visit Facebook, turn on the TV and other related activities, the battle begins for controlling what goes into your mind. Devoid of a panel of 'idiot lights' in your mind to send you warnings, you may excel in using technology, but fail in your school work.

Ways to Misuse Technology

I must admit that I, too, have wasted an incredible amount of time - too many hours in fact - doing mindless things with technology. I have learned from my mistakes. The strategies I am proposing are meant to assist in your quest not to become distracted. They have helped me get my act together.

1. One email can shave off at least an hour from your scheduled study time. The problem is, you have no idea where responding to a simple message is going to lead you. You get an email, you respond. The other person writes back. You may go back and forth, three or four times. Before you know it, one of you follows up with a phone call. By the time you put an end to the exchange, you have taken a whole hour, or more, from your studies.

You must combat the temptation to immediately respond to a call or email. If it does not pertain to your academic task, it can wait. Don't steal time away from your main commitment because your social life lingers in your inbox.

2. Another danger is that when we get absorbed in technology, we may treat our family and friends carelessly or disrespectfully. We tune out when they are speaking to us, we do not make eye contact, because we are busy scanning our messages.

Don't put gadgets over people. Treat the people who are part of your family and friendship network with genuine respect and interest. Texting or playing games instead of learning how to deepen relationships by communicating with those who are visiting is just plain disrespectful. Too many tech-absorbed young people get along better with technology than with other human beings. Don't get caught with that kind of deficiency.

3. There is nothing more disturbing to me than to witness a display of high-tech rudeness in a worship service. A cell phone goes off. It is the most sacred hour in the lives of believers.

The careless person frantically searches and finally locates the phone, which continues to ring before the disturbing interruption appears to end. Then the unbelievable happens. The guilty person presses a button on the device and actually checks to see who called! I guarantee it was not God calling.

Don't disturb events you attend with needless chatter and tech activities that belong in other areas of your life. Not paying attention results in sending negative signals that convey your lack of interest. You become a nuisance by not behaving in a respectful manner. Your demeanor is part of the ambience in sacred or cultural events. Shut the technology down. Respect others and yourself.

4. Another danger is surfing the Internet. Take note from a commenter who criticizes his own behavior in Steve Pavlina's online forum: "No matter what reason I turn my computer on, be it homework, or just to play games, I always end up wasting time on the Internet. I know I should be doing something more productive and interesting, but I just can't seem to get off. It's turned into a really bad habit that I can't break."

Why is the surfing distraction problematic for students? Dean Hunt, who is very familiar with high-tech interruptions, says:

"Research has shown that if you get distracted from a task for just five minutes, it can take another 15 minutes to get back into the zone. Put simply, get distracted just three times per hour for five minutes each time, and you will get almost nothing done."

5. Spending too much time with 'virtual friends' proves to be a huge distraction. Not only do real friendships suffer, but your homework does, too. Responding to these online distractions will keep you from doing your best work.

Chris Gaither notes the challenges faced by your generation are more complex than previous generations of students: "For decades, some kids have studied to music or while watching TV. But the computer's role as both an educational tool and a means for diversion all wrapped in the same package increases the allure of doing several things at once. AOL, for example, on Thursday released a search engine to help with homework, but it also offers plenty of time wasters, including instant messaging and video clips."

6. Multitasking while driving can be deadly. Teen drivers are most likely to be defined as "distracted drivers." One study documented that a driver using a cell phone was "four times more likely to get into an accident." The study also documented that "a driver text-messaging was six times more likely to get into an accident."

Furthermore, a nationwide survey reported that an estimated 45 percent of drivers below the age of 30, send text messages while driving. Teens call the practice, "driving while intexticated." No wonder the Economist article declared, "Certainly, texting while driving is one of the stupidest things a motorist can do."

7. The danger of becoming distracted adults is enhanced by the bad habits of your youth. The biggest distraction story so far has to do with the two airline pilots who became so focused on their computers that they flew over the city of their destination by over 150 miles. They were not paying attention to their job, which included the safety of their passengers and trying to arrive on time. They were working on their laptops, oblivious to their contract. These two pilots endangered the lives of hundreds of people. Northwest Airlines fired the pilots, apologized to the passengers and gave each one a $500 travel voucher to make amends.

The cost of distracted employees is huge. Here are some facts: One American study found that interruptions take up 2.5 hours of the average knowledge worker's day. This, it was estimated, costs the US economy $588 billion a year. When you interrupt and respond to interruptions through high-tech gadgets, the quality of your work suffers.

Distractions in one area are likely to lead to distractions in all other areas. Activate your distraction detectors in all aspects of your life!

Sexting Dangers

The sexting craze is a huge, dangerous distraction, which has paralyzed students on their journey to success. Sexting has gotten students expelled, in trouble with the law and, in some tragic cases, caused death.

Sexting is the practice of using the cell phone to send nude or seminude pictures to others. Young people are doing it all over the country and the world. Engaging in this type of behavior is problematic on many fronts. Sending such photos of children under 18 is against the law; moreover, if you are under 18 and are sending such pictures of yourself, it is still illegal. Not only is it illegal, it is extremely dangerous. Predators could create a false identity and target you online.

Sexting may be exciting, but it is dangerous and illegal. It is a potential tool for harassment or blackmail. What is sent for private consumption can become very public and permanent. Kate Shatzkin explains, "…Many kids don't grasp that the first two-letters in WWW stand for World Wide." Pictures intended for one person only often wind up on social websites or other tech venues. Someone in possession of your revealing photos could blackmail you. If caught, you will get in trouble with school authorities and with the law.

Sending a nude photo of a person as a prank may cause unbearable harm to the victim. The targeted person may experience persecution, a loss of reputation, peace of mind or even reasons for wanting to stay alive. That has happened in several cases.

A young woman, Jesse Logan of Ohio, sent her boyfriend nude pictures of herself. They later broke up. He became vindictive and circulated the photos to classmates who also circulated them to a wider audience. She was ridiculed, became the target of harassment and was labeled a "slut" and a "whore" by peers who had seen the photos.

She even went on a local TV program in Cincinnati to warn other students, "I just want to make sure that no one else will have to go through this again." Meanwhile, cyber bullies kept circulating her personal photos to students in four area high schools.

Jesse Logan sought to raise the awareness levels of students, warning them that sending private photos of love can turn ugly when loyalties shift and those you trusted decide to use technology to hurt you. Her studies suffered. She became truant. The taunting did not let up and she felt tortured.

On July 3, 2008, Jesse Logan committed suicide at 18 years old. Her story is the most tragic outcome of cyber bullying. She was a great kid who made a stupid mistake. Do not make the same mistake.

What makes sexting so prevalent is the fact that a lot of teens that are doing it claim to be bored;

sexting is exciting and graphic. Students can control their own cell phones and computers. They are curious and believe they can hide their actions from their parents and educators. In addition, these types of pictures give bragging rights. The age of Internet porn creates the illusion that going public with nakedness and sending images of body parts is acceptable. Millions of Internet porn websites reinforce the illusion.

The technology is powerful and the temptation to do what adults are doing creates incentives that jeopardize the currency of self-respect. The absence of being engaged in meaningful study and community projects that require time and talent leaves a void that gets filled up with frivolity online. The impulse to express love or hate in the moment with reckless abandonment very often wins over thinking before acting. Common sense and self-control take a back seat to clicking and texting with precision-driven and possibly destructive intensity.

STRATEGIES FOR SUCCESS

The brain is malleable. Just as it can be trained to be distracted it can be trained to pay attention.

Bryan Appleyard

a) Declare your independence from "Techism."

Addiction is wrong. Declare your independence from 'Techism,' - the process by which you are doing technology's bidding, rather than the other way around. Let high-tech resources assist your quest to become a free, balanced, informed, competent and educated person.

- Unplug your ears.

- Turn the phone off - you can review messages after finishing your school work.

- Give Facebook and other social media sites a time out.

- Use the technology – don't let it use you.

- Embrace your school work – let it take center stage in your life.

Do not become a victim of Techism. Control your time, interact with people of purpose and dare to boldly climb to the heights of academic excellence.

b) Avoid cyber-bullying and other forms of online social aggression and distress.

Rita, an international student, came to work for us. She soon learned through emails, chats and texting that she had been betrayed by her boyfriend. Worse, he was dating one of her friends. Upset and angry, she broke up with him.

However, she was even more furious with her former classmate for dating him!

Online aggression between the two women followed. Insults and counter insults were posted on social web sites, and hurled from one part of the world to the other. Links to supporters of each camp followed. The violent cyber exchanges caused seething anger, pain and tears for both parties. Scathing words and images were published at the click of a button and the virtual punching, slapping and biting ensued.

Both women have graduated from college and are happily married to respectful men in their lives. However, they have not made peace. Even years later, they revisit the posting of insults, keeping the flames of those distressful moments alive.

What is ironic is that today, both of them have an intense dislike for the lecherous creep who betrayed them.

Online aggression is almost impossible to erase. The technology that helps build friendships can also communicate hate. Do not allow the young, inexperienced person you are to ruin the reputation of the mature person you will become. Don't make your anger a permanent feature on YouTube or Facebook. It's far better to click off rather than tick off people with online aggression.

c) Learn how computer addiction works.

The literature uses different terms to describe the

process of paying too much attention to computer-generated activities:

- Internet distraction disorders
- Google computer addiction
- Virtual addiction
- Internet junkie
- Online porn addiction

Compulsive behavior that leads you to focus more on Facebook, for example, than on your family is dysfunctional. There are websites and formulas dedicated to assisting students in need of striking the balance between tech use and success in studying.

- My advice, start by activating your distraction detector. The following are other strategies that can act as deterrents:

- The computer has to come out of hiding; place it in a common area.

- Limit the amount of time you spend on the computer.

- Turn off the instant notification system that tells you you've got mail.

- Don't eat by the computer.

- Get out in the fresh air.

- Visit cultural events with peers and adults.

- Tutor younger students to do well in school.

- Volunteer in efforts that assist less fortunate human beings.

GETTING IT RIGHT CASE STUDY

The Internet and computer is often an escape from reality for teenagers who feel they do not fit in with the real world. Either in chat rooms or with games, the teenager can be whomever they choose to be. All it takes is a click of the mouse and they are in their fantasy world living out their dream life. Either in the form of a hero in a game to being somebody they are not in a chat room.

Jerome Carter

The reflections of JC, a high school student, are very revealing as he shares his story about overcoming distractions and getting it right. Read ahead:

My name is JC. I'm a Puerto Rican student who is attending high school in the Northwest. I relocated from Orlando, Florida. Even though I had physically moved, I was still emotionally glued to my friends from my JROTC class in Orlando. Like any teenager, I was less than thrilled to be leaving my friends, family, the school, and environment I had grown up in since the fourth grade. As I began to find my way in my new surroundings, I noticed something that could not be found in my new home – and that was diversity!

I was one of four Puerto Rican students in the largely white homogenous high school. I felt tense and isolated from what I was used to back home.

From the moment I started school, I felt like I did not belong. I felt I would not succeed as long as I was here. I had the thought of just leaving and returning to Orlando to be with everyone I loved. However, I was powerless to make that decision. When it came time for grades, they were less than satisfactory. I was in the red zone for failing my freshman year. To make matters worse, I had gotten into a physical fight with a Caucasian male who was racist toward me. He called me a bunch of anti-Latino racial slurs that I don't want to repeat. He disrespected me. I confronted him. He got in my face. He shoved. I pushed back. We fought. A teacher broke through the crowd of onlookers and separated us. On my way home, I remember feeling very bad and not wanting to be where I was not wanted. I felt trapped.

The feelings that came about with these racial problems left me wanting to go back to Florida even more and caused me to revert to a state of loneliness. While in this state, I would come home and get onto social networking sites, mostly MySpace.com.

I would chat with old classmates from JROTC. When they were no longer available to chat, I would play online games to pass the time. Watching TV kept me busy, too. The technology gave me the opportunity to escape from that awful reality. I could, with the click of my mouse, change the channels of my moods.

My musical situation had changed since I had moved. The music I loved to hear became scarce because the music channel BET and MTV3 were not available with my cable provider. The only way to stay current with new music was to shop around with MTV and VH1 to try to catch the times when my type of music was available on those channels. I spent a lot of time searching and listening to my music. I also watched TV. I was able to keep away from people I felt would not ever like me.

When semester classes changed, I met a teacher my spirit connected with who made me feel welcome. He was different. He was Samoan. As I got to know this teacher, I became more comfortable talking to him about my situation. He listened to me. When I told him I was failing classes and getting into fights because of my race, he set up a program to help others who felt like me.

I now had friends to study with and participate in social events with. He became our counselor and promised to help us throughout our high school careers.

This program would force me to become a better

person while bettering my mind and physique at the same time.

My new schedule was to work out for two hours every day and do my homework after that. With the program, I could not come home and talk on my cell phone, get on the computer or play video games irresponsibly; which were all the reasons I started to fail in the first place. My grades have improved dramatically.

Now that I am in my sophomore year, my body feels better and I have started playing football for my high school team. I have been told I have a lot of potential to become a better athlete if I can keep up my current regiment. Since the season has ended, I have gotten letters from Flagler College and Stetson University, which are both located in Florida, for football scholarships.

I am looking forward to continuing to earn excellent grades, participate in sports, honor my teacher and graduate from my new high school before going on to college. Technology will help me to achieve my dreams, not serve as a cause for my failure. Education will help me earn a living that will give me the opportunity to live where I want to be. Technology could have kept me back, trapped, failing and feeling sorry for myself. That is why I will no longer get distracted by online activities.

Finding my caring teacher and listening to him, about "putting first things first," has been the best thing that has happened to me.

CONCLUSION

Avoid getting distracted by high tech gadgets or alluring websites. The testimonials of people who got it wrong are plentiful and painful to read.

The tragic story of what happened to Jesse Logan should serve as a wakeup call to those engaged in sexting exchanges. Respect yourself and respect the privacy of others. Always assume that if you send compromising pictures of yourself via the Internet, they will be received and viewed by people whom you never intended to have access. Don't send them and you won't live to regret a stupid and potentially illegal act.

If you become addicted to high tech gadgets and the Internet, you have issues that need to be discussed with a competent professional counselor.

Remember, technology is a good thing and can help facilitate your journey to the head of the class if you exercise discipline and maintain focus. Use technology wisely. Don't allow the wide array of distractions to derail your quest to be the best.

STEP 9

Stop Pursuing Logical Paths to Wrong Destinations

Logic is the art of going wrong with confidence.

Joseph Wood Krutch

WHY YOU MUST GET IT RIGHT!

Jim Green put it best when he said, "We do things that are not correct; then we invent logical sounding reasons to justify our actions, and then believe our invented reasons for what we did."

Believing your own lies is a trap you must avoid. The fact is that we engage more in rationalizing than in being rational. When you stray from your goal to excel, your behavior demands an explanation. That's when the temptation to spin a tale to justify abandoning your responsibilities takes hold.

Failing to look beyond the urgent desires of the moment can have disastrous consequences. As students, you have to be careful not to pursue immediate gratification then justify why your actions were more important than studying.

Inventing a logical excuse to rationalize what you did, rather than what you needed to do, will not help you to excel.

What Is Logical Is Not Always Correct

That's right. What is logical is not always correct. Is it possible to have smart, logical explanations for actions that promote academic failure? Yes! When you act impulsively to satisfy a pressing desire, without any serious consideration for the negative impact the action may have, the chances are you will come up with a logical, self-convincing rationalization.

A student once engaged me in a logical discussion regarding car ownership. He spoke of the merits of purchasing a new car over a used one.

"Isn't it true when a person buys an old car, he may be buying someone else's problems?" he asked.

"Yes," I said. The answer seemed obvious.

He then proceeded to tell me that to avoid making the disastrous mistake of buying someone else's problem; he was going to purchase a new car. His uncle would sign for the loan.

Then he added, "I am taking a year off from my college studies."

"Oh. Why is that?" I countered.

"Because I can't afford to pay for my new car and go to school at the same time," he concluded.

It all made sense to him. He thought it through and sought confirmation from his sociology professor. He rationalized that since he did not want to buy someone else's problem, he would have to buy a new car. He focused solely on the purchase of a car as the issue and failed to connect this decision with his broader, more long-term goal of completing his college studies.

One wonders if he gave any consideration to the hidden costs involved with the purchase of a new vehicle. You have to buy a city sticker, plates, insurance and possibly an alarm system and extended warranty. High-tech gadgets like GPS systems and top-of-the-line speakers also increase the cost. Not to mention regular maintenance and fuel.

This student did not care to discuss other alternatives regarding his transportation predicament. We could have talked about using public transportation, carpooling or exploring creative ways of buying a used car while minimizing the possibility of inheriting someone else's lemon. He failed to think critically and connect the dots. The leading question regarding the purchase of other people's problems was a set up for me to agree with his logical argument for buying a new car.

Had my student delayed gratification and completed his schooling; he could have landed a professional job with benefits and been in a better position to purchase a car in the future. By putting his studies on hold, he was risking his academic career. To this day, I don't know if he returned to school. He never communicated with me again.

Reflecting on what he did brings a sour taste to my mouth. He used me as part of his ploy to find a logical reason for putting his educational journey on hold. I take great exception to any student taking my time and using my intellectual resources to justify quitting school.

Being on Your Own May Keep You from Owning Your Own Place

Life may be intolerable where you are. You believe the only way out is to get a place of your own. Since it takes money to put a deposit down on an apartment, pay rent and purchase the essentials, you think you have to quit school and go to work. The argument is compelling. Staying in school will simply not do; at least for the moment. Convinced, you are ready to take the plunge and it feels right. But is it?

Let us look beyond the conclusion you might draw by following the logical path just outlined. Quitting school temporarily so you can work and pay for your own place may sound logical at face value. But, as the saying goes, "The medicine may be worse than the disease."

You might convince yourself that leaving school is temporary and you will be able to get back into the groove when you can afford it. But, consider that returning to study with a generation that is high tech savvy, disciplined and focused on how to study, while you have grown intellectually flabby, may not be as easy as you think.

When work competes with school, your commitment to education is compromised. Work will connect you to new friendships with people who are not engaged in study. New social obligations will occupy your nights. Study habits will most likely be replaced by hanging out with friends, dating (with constant privacy since you have your own place), watching videos and more time on the computer. This lifestyle, 'free' of homework exercises, writing papers and preparing for exams, may contribute to your becoming permanently distracted from the goal of pursuing formal education.

What will happen to your plans to finish school? They will vanish. Gone will be the benefits of an education and the challenge of abstract thinking, chasing ideas, embracing concepts, organizing thought patterns, brainstorming with study partners, pursuing comparative frameworks of thought and revising drafts into clearer, sharper, more meaningful essays.

Don't put your education on hold; stay on the case until you graduate. Refuse to believe your justifications for getting out of a temporarily stressful situation to possibly create a permanent one.

What Loves and Fulfills Can also Suffocate and Destroy

When is loving and becoming intimate with someone who loves you in return a bad thing? When it derails your need to first become educated and develop your toolkit for successful life skills. Education will qualify you to seek employment with salary and benefits. You will learn how to avoid pitfalls that pull couples apart and guide you to understand that the young person you are today has no business making decisions for the matured, experienced adult you will become tomorrow.

I believe in long-term relationships because love is sweet and intimacy fulfilling. The desire to be held, hugged and embraced is on point with normal human needs and desires. So, what's the problem? Timing!

Abandoning your education to pursue matters of the heart is foolhardy. Becoming romantically entangled and sexually active at the wrong time is one path fraught with major dangers. The fear of pregnancy and disease, compounded by the worries that come with a complex relationship, make this choice particularly challenging for a young, maturing individual.

It is exhausting and emotionally expensive!

Doing something that feels good may make sense in a world that promotes a "just do it!" philosophy. However, looming large on the walls of high school hallways are signs that warn: "If you go all the way, you won't get very far." All the logical explanations you invent to justify doing what is wrong, before you are educated and mature, cannot get you out of the jams that may occur.

There are alternatives to the "just do it" philosophy. Release pent-up energy through sports, exercise and hard physical work. Socialize through group activities. Make friends with peers who are serious about their academic success. Resist visiting websites that fuel your sexual fantasies and encourage you to use and be used by other people in the name of 'love.'

Climbing to the head of the class takes time, hard work and creative energy. Loving someone and becoming intimate with a caring soul mate is great if you have enough education and networks with wiser, more experienced mentors who can serve as trusted guides in your journey to excel in life.

The Jobs that Put Money in Your Pocket Can Keep You Poor

Growing up broke is one heck of a motivating

factor for wanting to go to work. In the old days, before credit cards, you were somebody when you had "change jingling in your pocket." I grew up on welfare. My pockets were always silent. We were very poor. I hated my circumstances. I just wanted to be like other kids, whose parents had cars, went on vacations and received gifts for their birthdays and holidays.

The television was the high-tech gadget of my day. If you were lucky and had a friend who had a TV, you would spend a lot of time watching it at their house. But, if not, that meant standing outside a store that sold them and watching from the sidewalk. When we heard that Peter Pan was going to be on TV, my brother and I begged our mom to let us watch it in front of Mr. Siegel's TV and appliance store down on Intervale Avenue in the Bronx. She agreed, even though it premiered on a cold night in November.

My mom bundled us up as best she could because the store was quite a few blocks away. We rushed to get a choice position by the window.

When the show finally started, we were heartbroken! It was Peter Pan all right, except it was a live show from a Broadway production. We desperately wanted to see the official Walt Disney cartoon version. We could not afford the 20 cents to go to the Ace movie theater when it was showing. Crest fallen and ashamed of our status, we said as little as possible about the whole affair. Our mom was just happy to get us back safely and earlier than expected.

Not having easy access to high-tech gadgets means you are an outcast. You don't belong. It's an awful feeling. Once, when my mother started to see a man and he wanted to move into our apartment, he met with my teenage brothers and me. He asked if we would consent.

We said, "Sure, if you buy us a TV!"

He bought us a 21-inch, black and white Philco TV, and moved in. That's how hungry we were.

We negotiated for our mom to live with this dude we didn't know just so we could have what other kids had. Our misplaced desire for material things would lead to disaster. The man was a thug and proved to be a horrible father to the daughter who was conceived in that relationship. He failed to become the father-figure we so desperately needed. As teens, we did not have enough information as to what the future would bring. We just wanted a TV.

Growing up, we never had furniture that matched. My mother procured our family wardrobe from the Dorcas Center, which was run by Seventh-Day Adventists. I will never forget the subway rides from Queens to the Bronx with paper bags full of used shoes and clothing. I was both grateful and humiliated by the process.

I never owned a new sports jacket or a suit. If I had brand new jeans and a shirt, the shoes were old and worn. If I had a haircut and new shoes, then the jeans needed to be replaced. I remember my brother had to stuff toilet paper in the shoes that were too big for him. Since I was the youngest of the boys, the hand-me-down shirts and slacks were often too large for me and I was sick of it.

At age 17, quitting school was a no brainer. I wanted to find my place in the sun. I wanted to buy new stuff. I wanted money, adventure and a car – and I wanted them immediately. I was just plain tired of not having anything. So, I decided to join the military to get the whole 'enchilada.'

It was a natural avenue to a quick buck and the material goodies of the time. Back then, all you needed was your parents' permission. My mom agreed.

"Not so fast, young man," the warning was on point and on time. "You are not joining anything until you graduate from high school and college."

My coach and mentor, Mary Yamazaki, caught my attention. She persuaded me to start connecting the dots. She kept me from crashing into dead-end jobs requiring a high school diploma or less. I am forever grateful that she interrupted my journey. She motivated me to complete high school, graduate from college, and finish graduate school.

Her advice is relevant today in view of our high tech environment and global economy. Getting a job without benefits at minimum pay is simply not enough. Developing your brains, so you can earn a salary as a professional, requires delaying gratification, sitting on your urges and investing in the future. To go from poverty to the professions you must first cross a bridge called books. I know, because earning minimum pay would have kept me in poverty.

Investing in Education Can Open the World of Wonder and Work

There are many benefits and values to being educated. Today, I have the resources to help my family, retire with dignity and be generous to causes I believe in. I, alongside my wife, own our home in Chicago, an oceanfront villa in Puerto Rico and another property on Guam overlooking the Pacific Ocean. We take a vacation to Hawaii every year and I have had the privilege to travel in Africa, Europe, Asia, the Middle East, Oceana, and throughout the Americas.

I do not mention my material possessions and my travels to boast, nor to provide false hopes. I only wish to share that without an education and friendship with those who understand how to save and invest, my vacations would have been impossible. My hope is to get you to consider how education can add to your quest. Teaming up with educated people can enhance the quality of your life.

My wife, Laura, is the one who knows how to make sense of the economic resources in our family.

However, I could not have attracted her to become my soul mate without the qualifications to lecture, teach and consult in the forums that brought us together as equal educated professionals. Between the two of us, we have 44 years of formal education!

Please be careful not to take shortcuts to get material things at the expense of educating your mind. You need to find a wise adult or two who care about your future and have your best interests at heart. Give them permission to get in your face. Seek their counsel on how to get the education you need, in spite of your economic setbacks. Let them advise you on what steps to take in following logical paths to the right destinations.

Adult counselors got in my face and advised me to earn my diploma and degree before getting married, buying a car and traveling. I listened. Through education, my fortunes were transformed. Don't quit or postpone your quest to excel. Stay the course. Your fortunes can multiply through more education.

Reflect on the African proverb: "For tomorrow belongs to the people who prepare for it today."

I read a great book that reveals how people who work in certain jobs can't get out of poverty. In her

book, Nickel and Dimed: On (Not) Getting by in
America, Barbara Ehrenreich reveals what life is
like for people who work in menial jobs. Read it
before you decide to quit school to find a job in
hopes of returning to school when things improve.
If you can, get student loans and finish your
formal education.

Wealth Devoid of an Education Can Be Lethal

A few months ago, I visited Bermuda. My flight
was pleasant. Sitting across the aisle from me
was the actor Michael Douglas. For most of the
flight from Miami to Bermuda, he was engrossed
in Tom Friedman's Hot, Flat, and Crowded. It
struck me that even though this man is part of
Hollywood royalty, is enormously wealthy and
seemingly has it all, he still continues to read
serious literature. It affirms everything I try to
teach. Learning never stops. Even if you get to
the top of the food chain, stay abreast of current
events and continue figuring out how to become
part of the solution. Don't stop reading.

The landing was smooth and getting through
customs was a breeze. They welcome tourists
and business people easily.

The pound and the dollar were at par with each
other, so shopping and purchasing food and
sundries was very easy. My hotel
accommodations were exquisite. Framed with
aesthetic beauty and elegance at every turn, the

flowers, manicured lawns and landscaping gave me the sense that Bermuda is one giant botanical garden by the sea.

The total absence of poverty, run down neighborhoods, abandoned cars and urban decay was jarring to my senses. Diverse faces in all places are part of the social fabric and tropical ambience. I grew up on welfare in the mean streets of poor urban cities; here, young people live in opulence. How fortunate for the citizens of this country who live in this marvelous place.

Dr. Jeffery Brown, who hosted my visit, shared a joke that circulates in Bermuda: "One homeless person tells another, 'Please watch my stuff until I get back from my cruise'."

Money Does Not Equal Wealth

I had the time of my life. My presentations were featured on TV. I was asked to visit classrooms and speak to assemblies of faculty, staff and students.

I was able to collaborate with visionary educational leaders and challenge students to stay in school and graduate. Sharing my story, from Harlem to Harvard, proved the highlight for many students living sheltered lives in beautiful Bermuda. However, all did not go well in paradise.

Most of the students I spoke to were passionate

about furthering their education. However, some young people resisted the idea of continuing beyond high school because they stand to inherit expensive houses and property from their parents.

As they put it, "We are going to have money. We don't need a lot of education."

Yes, they will inherit choice properties in one of the most gorgeous places on Earth, but they confuse having income and property with having enough resources to make it in life.

Money does not equal wealth; religion does not equal spirituality; nor does a house equal a home; or a group of relatives equal a family. Material possessions devoid of education can be a lethal combination.

Learning from Winners of Millions Who Went Broke

There are tragic stories of people who have won millions in the lottery and lost everything. Jack Whitaker won $315 million in the Powerball lottery jackpot; today he is broke.

Other winners who lost include Suzane Mullins, William 'Bud' Post and Janite Lee. How did they use up all that money? Their lack of education, wisdom and networks of purpose-driven friends frustrated their ability to learn that money is not the answer to life's problems.

The most logical and correct step you can take is to become educated. Other like-minded people will become attracted to you and vice versa. Solving urgent problems and making your resources work for you require an education.

My problem was being poor and not having enough material resources; your problem may be having too many material things. In both cases, education is essential for making a positive difference in your life and in society. Education – not just schooling – will bring balance to those with too little or too much.

You must seek understanding and wisdom and the company of those who follow the path to the right destinations with education.

What Is Funny and Entertaining Can also Be Harmful

You must ponder the consequences of following the logical path of using debilitating humor about some groups, including your own, as a source of entertainment. What is logical is not always correct.

Telling anti-group jokes, which demeans, mocks and pokes fun at different groups, will never uplift the spirits of others. Building strong identity bonds with members of your own group at the expense of stigmatizing others may promote distrust and make you insensitive to people's feelings.

Getting applause by beating up others with cruel jokes poisons relationships. It's going to be hard for you to laugh at members of "out-groups" and then welcome them for team projects in school.

At this crucial time in our history, the need for unity based on an appreciation of diversity is most urgent. Laughter at the expense of people simply leads to a wrong destination. View others with respect.

Team up with youth from different backgrounds to win championships. Reject hate acts, whether expressed in anger or humor. Join or start organizations in your school that promote understanding by reducing prejudice.

STRATEGIES FOR SUCCESS

There are two kinds of failures: those who thought and never did, and those who did and never thought.

Dr. Laurence J. Peter

a) Resist material symbols of success, get educated and qualified to succeed.

Hollow people are driven by what is on sale and what glitters. They will always chase after the newest high tech toys to feed their egos. Refuse to become a commodity of a materialistic society.

Don't pursue cars, brand name clothes and gadgets as a way of showing how valuable you are.

There are no short cuts. Don't hustle people to buy expensive stuff on credit so you can act as though you are somebody. The more money you spend on things today, the more you have to work to pay those things off tomorrow.

Stop wanting the symbols of success before you have educated yourself to be successful.

Stay humble and in pursuit of knowledge and wisdom. Avoid hanging around with pretentious people and don't be pretentious yourself. Inspire your peers to join in your quest to climb to the head of the class. Spend time reading to improve your grades and see what you can do to graduate quicker.

Excel in school to succeed in life. You will become a symbol of great value by what you will achieve, not by the things you own, drive, communicate with or wear.

b) **Don't quit school to take a dead-end job in hopes of returning – it's too risky.**

Stresses at home can lead you to believe that putting school on hold while you work and become independent is the way to go.

However, working at jobs that pay wages commensurate with your worth in the marketplace may barely be enough to meet your new obligations. Wages after taxes, transportation, parking fees, food and other expenses may fall short of your expectations.

A lot of hidden costs will leave you owing money rather than saving at the end of a pay period. So think about where you might be headed before you reason that leaving home is going to be better. It might not be. What sounds logical is not always correct.

It's best for you to stay put and weather the discomforts of home while you continue to do well in school. Wait until you are truly able to go out into a better tomorrow with your formal educational program completed. Meanwhile, help out around the house; make your bed and study with focus. Those actions tend to get your parents off your back.

In addition, it might be revealing to speak with people close to you who have interrupted their schooling. Find out how many returned as planned. Take notes, especially from those who thought of returning and did not. Ask them what they would do if they had a chance to do it again. You might be surprised at their insights born out of real life experience.

Put up with the short-term stress at home until you graduate, rather than the long-term stress of wishing you had graduated.

c) **Keep romantic entanglements from suffocating your goal to excel.**

Romantic relationships can cause you to pull away from your studies and cook up logical stories to cover your tracks. These relationships use up a lot of the creative energy, time and other resources necessary to do well in school.

Have you ever fallen head over heels in love with someone and begun to float in la-la land? Soon, all you can think about is your sweetheart. Phone conversations, texting and photo exchanges put every other commitment you've made on hold.

Sexting and compromising webcam exchanges may appear to be normal expressions of love in the tech rich environment we live in, but before you know it, you're in harm's way. You will take risks and do things that, in retrospect, will be seen as dangerous, stupid and unbalanced. Emails and Twitter messages that promise complete surrender are sent back and forth. Doing what comes naturally can be a logical next step. One argument later, the relationship might explode or melt away. Everything you did that was motivated by the feelings of the moment can come back to haunt you.

When you break up, you ask yourself, "What in the world was I thinking about?"

Don't mess up your priorities. Finish school first, then fall in love and team up with someone who has also finished school, and pool your resources to improve the quality of your life. My wife, Laura, and I did just that.

To paraphrase a famous line from Sammi Smith's country and western song, Help Me Make It through the Night, "Don't let the devil take tomorrow because tonight you need a friend."

d) Laugh to heal, not to harm.

Work at seeking greater understanding, not more divisiveness. Exercise leadership in requesting class assignments that analyze and evaluate media programming that poison relationships between groups. Learn to laugh with others, not at others. Conduct research on what constitutes healthy, uplifting and inclusive humor, then compare those principles with what constitutes debilitating and offensive humor. Diversity is part of our collective legacy. Be a part of what helps heal rather than what cheapens our dignity and humanity. What's funny is not always worth repeating.

Humor can be a healing force in life. A sense of humor can add value to our lives. After all, laughter is the best medicine. Children love clowns. Great humorists are always in demand. The most popular teachers and public speakers are those who are gifted with a sense of humor. So laugh and recycle funny tales that are worth repeating. Just be careful you don't cause injury by telling tales that poison relationships. No matter the logic that convinces you it's proper and you don't mean any harm, claiming, "It's just a joke," when in doubt, don't.

GETTING IT RIGHT CASE STUDY

No, no, you're not thinking; you're just being
logical.

Niels Bohr

Dr. Rosita Lopez says it best: "Once one has
been on a series of wrong paths, getting on the
right one can be daunting." Get educated first
and your chances of excelling in life will be
greatly enhanced. Dr. Lopez shares her story:

As a Puerto Rican female growing up in Chicago,
my experiences with schools, teachers and the
system left me wondering about whether I should
even try to belong in a world dominated by
English speakers. When I first started classes, I
was put in the first grade because I was too old
for kindergarten. I remember how excited I was
about going to school. My mother fixed my long
black hair into a beautiful set of braids and
dressed me in handmade dresses native to our
island. When I wasn't sure about something, I
learned to stay quiet, observe and study it until I
figured it out. I spent many days being quiet.

My mother already taught me most of what they
were teaching in school. Subsequently, I was
ahead and on the honor roll regularly. However,
this learning experience would also expose me to
the cruelty shown to those considered "different."
One day, my class was standing in line waiting to

enter the bathroom. On the hunt for students with lice and other signs of poor hygiene, a couple of teachers began walking around the line, sniffing our heads. This behavior puzzled me. They continued their "sniffing" research. Every so often, they would comment to each other.

One of them approached me and picked up the tip of my braid, abruptly letting it fall as if to be careful not to make too much contact. I think I passed, because they continued down the line. I remember feeling insignificant and dirty. I was "sniffed," commented on. As years passed, I began feeling indifferent, no longer the daughter who could read and write in two languages. I began to feel ashamed of my parents, of how I looked and of being Puerto Rican.

High school was the least supportive educational environment I had yet to encounter. It was a place of misery, with little respect for the acquisition of knowledge. I began finding excuses for not going to school. I never joined clubs or sports teams and never even went to the prom. It seemed logical to leave school. In my mind, I had already dropped out! I convinced my parents to let me follow a path to the mountains of Puerto Rico where my grandparents lived. I took time to reflect and replenish my spirit, but I found that escaping was the wrong path to follow. I missed my family and soon returned home. I was ashamed of not graduating with my class. My friends would ask if I was at the graduation and my response was always, "Sure, I saw you there, you just never saw me, but I was there."

After I dropped out of high school, my journey took me through a series of paths that seemed logical, but again led me to wrong destinations. I married a person I did not love. I had a son, who was a blessing, but before long, I became a single parent with no income or education. I looked around me and saw girls with babies they could not support or handle. They looked tired and old. It was clear this was not a good destination. I had to do something. It was then I decided to take my GED. Shortly thereafter, I found a job at St. Elizabeth's Hospital. I learned more in my experiences at the hospital than I ever had in any school. I worked in various departments throughout St. Elizabeth's and met many people who inspired me. However, something was still missing.

Once one has been on a series of wrong paths, getting on the right one can be daunting. I was a single mother working full time with a growing desire to become educated. In retrospect, returning to school at the University of Illinois at Chicago was the most difficult part of my formal education. Adding school to my list of responsibilities meant the forfeiture of any spare time I had. On top of that, I wasn't confident that I could handle the assignments, especially the math classes.

However, my algebra teacher offered to help and after a few weeks of tutoring, he said I had a gift for mathematics! It had been a long time since a teacher had said something positive to me. It was all I needed to gain a little self-confidence and not give up. It was during these years I decided to become a teacher. I wanted to be the best teacher I could be! Education and determination was the formula I needed to succeed.

Finally, I was on the right path toward becoming an educated professional! I developed an insatiable appetite for education. My BA wasn't enough. The master's program introduced me to ideas I had never imagined. I brought new methods and strategies into the classroom. Some things worked, while others did not. I bounced ideas off of other teachers to see if they had a better response. I found myself reading and researching constantly as I tried to figure out ways to make methods applicable to my own students. The very few bilingual materials at that time were dull and of poor quality, so I learned to translate materials from English to Spanish so my students could also enjoy them.

After graduation, I heard about a doctoral program at Northern Illinois University.

I decided to explore the possibilities, but it seemed like such a faraway dream. A friend asked me, "Why do you need a doctorate? Won't you be overly qualified for jobs?" A family member asked, "Haven't you taken enough time away from your family? Where are you going with this?" I couldn't respond to their questions and concerns. It's ironic that these naysayers would be so vocal when I was finally turning my life around for the better – they were absent when I was on the wrong path. I turned to my parents for advice. My mother was always a source of inspiration and encouragement. My father stood his ground on education; it was the best thing I could accomplish, no one could take it away from me. I seized the opportunity.

Once enrolled in the program, my fellow classmates and I were challenged, enlightened and empowered. I worked harder than I had ever worked in my life. I must admit that there were days I cursed the program because I was so exhausted from all the course requirements. However, I moved forward, completed the task, finished my dissertation and graduated! Pursuing my education was the right path I needed to take.

It has led me to a series of destinations that have empowered me as a teacher and as a professional. And the older I got, the better it looked on me! Many wonderful opportunities have emerged. I have had the good fortune of meeting inspiring leaders and now understand that success is a journey that never rests.

CONCLUSION

Resist using logic to justify long-term bad decisions. Finish school and graduate several times over before deciding the line of work you want to do. Work in dead-end jobs to earn money so you can study. Whether you have very little or a lot of material possessions, you need to become educated to improve the quality of your life and assist in helping solve urgent problems in our world.

You can hurt people through careless, vicious, debilitating humor. No matter how funny the punch line, it's not wise to circulate offensive jokes that poison relationships.

The young person you are today should not be making permanent decisions for the matured and educated adult you will become tomorrow. Avoid getting cozy in the emotional, intimate area of your life before you have matured and received counsel from wise, more experienced and caring adults in your life.

STEP 10

Honor Loved Ones
With Your Academic Success

Education is a loan to be repaid with the gift of
self.

Lady Bird Johnson

WHY YOU MUST GET IT RIGHT!

Deciding that you are worthy of the best is the
most powerful incentive for wanting to excel. To
do right for others, you must first want to do right
for you. Champion your self-worth by learning
more. Having a healthy self-esteem and high self-
regard, however, does not mean becoming self-
absorbed and selfish. Loving self first will lead to
loving others best.

Lucille Ball was fond of saying, "Love yourself first
and everything else falls into line. You really have
to love yourself to get anything done in this
world."

This step is about graduations, gratitude and
giving back to those who have invested in your
success. I want to challenge you to become a
lifelong learner. Keep preparing to make a
difference as you establish your identity as an

educated professional. Graduate from high school. Then, inspire loved ones to stand up and cheer as you enroll for more formal education. Continue to grow your problem-solving skills. Strain every nerve to achieve excellence in your course work. Only by sacrificing will you get it done. Remember, nothing worthwhile is ever easy.

Let's visit the first and most important rite of passage, high school graduation. The following narrative is written for two reasons; reflection for those who have gone through it and anticipation for those who have yet to experience this meaningful event. Wherever you are in your journey, let graduating from high school serve as a launching pad for your future academic success.

Anticipate Taking Center Stage at Your High School Graduation

Repay the loan of education – make your first installment payment graduating from high school. Invite those who invested in your success to the ceremony.

Dress smartly for the occasion. Show up early. Wear your cap and gown with pride. Make sure the tassel is on the right side of your cap. Silence your cell phone and resist the urge to talk, tweet or text during the ceremony. Pay attention. Don't let this moment pass you by.

As the formal program gets underway, everyone will stand. The principal and special guests will enter and make their way up to the platform. The sound of music will signal that something of great importance is about to happen. It does. In full regalia, you and the other members of the senior class will make a dramatic entrance into the auditorium. It's time for you to own the room. Stride in unison with your peers toward your reserved seats to the beat of the traditional graduation song, War March of the Priests by Felix Mendelssohn. The tune will remain embedded in your memory forever, for it has framed your graduation – your first publicly recognized major civic accomplishment.

In this place, on this date, at this event, change has come to your life. You will never be labeled a high school dropout or loser. You have excelled. Good for you. Embrace the moment.

When all the graduates have entered and located their seats, the music will stop. Remain standing. Face the flag. The Pledge of Allegiance will follow. A classmate will lead in the singing of the Star Spangled Banner. This is very appropriate. Education prepares you for responsible citizenship. Everyone present will then be directed to sit down. A program will be by your seat. Pick it up. You will be able to follow the flow of the day's agenda. Nothing on this day has been left to chance, for this is a defining moment on your journey toward maturity and greater responsibility.

The principal will welcome everyone – especially the graduates. Dignitaries will be recognized and greeted from the podium. A musical, cultural, or artistic performance by one of your peers will likely enhance the celebratory mood. Honor the president and the valedictorian of your class with proper decorum as they deliver their speeches. The speaker of the hour will be introduced. Pay attention to the commencement address.

Gleam memorable pieces of advice from what's being said to guide your journey through life.

A striking line from a commencement address I heard still bounces inside my head. It goes like this: "Don't wait for the storm to pass, learn to dance in the rain."

When tempted to slack off, those words have a way of motivating me to get back on track. I am challenged to stay in the thick of struggles; not to seek safety at the expense of relevance. Which lines will you retain from your speaker?

Get ready for the big moment – receiving your diploma! First, you must applaud the superstars and recognized champions among the graduates. Some will receive scholarships. If you are like me, the first in the family to do so, graduating will be a big deal. The name of each graduating senior will be printed in the program. Follow the list to become alert as to when your name will be called. Follow your row of classmates to the front. A teacher will let you know when to start walking toward center stage.

When your name is called and you get the nod, make your move toward the spotlight; you've earned it. Remember, all eyes are on you. So walk tall and take deliberate steps to receive your diploma.

Don't be startled or embarrassed by members of your family and friends shouting and clapping loudly when your formal name is called. Shake hands with the official handing you your precious certificate. Pause. Someone will be taking your photo to capture the moment; smile.

No doubt a video will also document the occasion. Don't do anything foolish on stage for cheap laughs. This moment also belongs to the loving, supportive members of your network of investors. Treat the occasion with solemnity. Take a deep breath, walk to your row and sit down. Wow, you did it – and your moment at center stage has been captured by media and documented forever!

Upon receipt of their diplomas, all graduates will be directed to move the tassels to the left side of your caps. This small ritual signals that you are no longer high school students. A former graduate who once sat where you are now seated and who now has an important position in society will recognize you as alums of the school. She or he will make a pitch for you to support your school in the future. Agree to become a member of the Alumni Association and a booster for your school. Giving back to your school is another form of repayment of the loan of education.

A hearty congratulations to the members of the graduating class from the principal will be followed by caps in the air, shouts of glee and joy, spontaneous embracing by close friends, palm slapping – this very acceptable, blissful "mini-disturbance" signals the euphoria that meeting educational goals can bring. Friends and family members who are physically able will spring to their feet and give you a standing ovation. Tears of happiness will baptize the event for some of your nurturers. They will hug each other, knowing that your success is part of their reward. They recognize you have taken a giant step toward becoming independent. They will be happy and scared for you.

Marching out to greet well-wishers will be the very last time you will participate in a collective event with your classmates. Relish the moment. The bittersweet experience of graduating and leaving a familiar world for new adventures in living and learning is reaching its climax.

Outside, pose for still photos and video recordings of the event. Images will flow from phone cameras to Facebook and other social media networks in a flash. Flowers, balloons and pats on the back will abound on the school grounds.

Express your gratitude with hugs, kisses and vigorous handshakes with family and friends.

Jennifer Lopez adds value: "If you love someone, don't wait till tomorrow to tell him/her. Maybe that next day will never come at all."

So get busy expressing those words of love to those you honor with your graduation. Salute your teachers as well. Embrace your classmates. Bid them farewell as you smile through the tears of memories that will last a lifetime.

Make peace with someone you have had words with during the course of your journey. Seek forgiveness when you have done wrong and forgive when you have been wronged. Let this graduation exercise be a form of cleansing and let it usher a new season of grace in your spirit. Education allows you to reason together as opposed to beating each other up with insults or the threat of physical violence.

Let the serenity-driven disposition of emerging educated professionals replace the resentments of a less mature past and the bumpy relationships of yesterday.

This process will make you remember your graduation as the time you left the cocoon of a less developed self and morphed into a royal monarch – a more actualized, generous person. Making peace with others will qualify you to become your own best friend.

Enjoy the sweets, punch and finger food

available. Return the cap and gown to the proper officials. Keep the tassel as a memento and never forget the saying: "The tassel's worth the hassle!"

Later, try to visit the resting places of loved ones no longer with you who would be beaming with joy at your accomplishments. Take them flowers, if only in your thoughts. That night, enjoy the music, pose for more pictures, open gifts, eat and drink your favorite festive foods. Text pictures of the celebration to those in your inner circles of trust. Post them in your social networks as well. Through the magic of technology and the mini cams attached to computers, visit those far away to share in the celebration.

Be generous with your expressions of gratitude. Let the meaningful people in your life express joy in your accomplishments via the technology that is such a part of your life, while the festive moment is hot.

Pause and tell the younger kids who look up to you that they, too, must graduate. The next day, frame your diploma and hang it on the picture wall close to your graduation portrait and tassel. Showcase your scholarly trophies for everyone to see that you have begun to pay your investors by your success in school.

Why Graduating More Than Once Is Essential

Now that I've described and added meaning and

reasons as to why graduating from high school is pivotal to your success, don't stop learning. Commit to completing or graduating from post-secondary institutional programs or degrees several times over. Here's why:

1. The more formal educational programs you complete, the better your chances for working and thriving in our changing, highly technical society.

2. A high school diploma followed by a college degree is essential to the quest of becoming a more informed citizen and the search for meaningful relationships.

3. Skill sets for communicating more effectively with subject matter experts are greatly enhanced through more education.

4. As an educated leader and volunteer in community and civic duties, you will be a tremendous asset.

5. Nurturing and developing the talents of the younger generation in your family networks will necessitate that you continue to increase your formal knowledge.

6. For greater effectiveness in teaching, coaching and mentoring, you must become a role model who walks the talk when it comes to graduating more than once.

7. Leading change in our diverse world and society requires comparative frameworks,

more languages and competencies for making coalitions of interest across identity lines that benefit from more formal education.

Simply put, the gift of self demands it and the world of work requires it. Don't stop pursuing more formal education. With it, life will not be easy. Imagine what life will be like without it.

It's not just about how much you can get out of more education, but how much you can give in return. Education may very well be the gift that keeps on giving.

Tom Brokaw says, "You are educated. Your certification is in your degree. You may think of it as the ticket to the good life. Let me ask you to think of an alternative. Think of it as your ticket to change the world."

The Benefits and Values of Graduating from Accredited Programs

Plan to attend and graduate from degree granting institutions. Be distrustful of investing monies to earn certificates from institutions that fail to qualify you for job opportunities. Talk with former students before investing time and money toward those programs. Seek credentials from two-year and four-year degree granting institutions. Many jobs simply require that you have earned a degree. When you graduate from college, employers will take note, knowing that you:

- attended classes

- budgeted your time

- completed your projects

- worked well in teams

- increased your vocabulary

- met deadlines

- invested time and money in your success

- universalized your world view

- perfected your skills for using technology effectively

- learned to respect the scientific method of logical thinking

- exercised and increased your competencies to live healthier lives

- grew in your capacity to respect diverse points of views

- volunteered for student activities

- learned to dress for success

- sharpened skills for joining diverse, mission-driven work teams

Develop those cultural skill sets. Improve the places in which we live, work, shop, learn, govern, recreate and worship. Become a citizen who pays your fair share of taxes. Give back by volunteering and networking as an educated member of your community. Flee from the mindset that you are entitled to coast, receive benefits and give nothing in return. Complete your school projects. Don't stop learning and graduate!

From Grunt Work to Mind Work and What I Learned about Respect

Before I worked with my mind as a professional, I had to earn a living with my hands and back as a common laborer.

When I was a kid, my brothers and I delivered groceries for lady shoppers from the local A&P market to their apartments in the South Bronx. We sold sacks of Long Island potatoes for 50 cents each, by shouting out to tenement residents from the back of a truck.

We traveled to rough neighborhoods all over the city and hauled these huge sacks up long flights of stairs in tall buildings without elevators for mere tips; and some customers wouldn't! We returned home, hoarse and tired, but had loose change in our pockets to supplement the meager welfare check my mom got.

I picked fruits and tomatoes in agricultural fields in New Jersey. I took care of thousands of chickens in a dirty, smelly poultry farm full of flies and manure. I washed dishes in a Mexican restaurant in Chicago.

The summer I turned 17, I worked as an orderly in a hospital in the suburbs – my duties included washing and drying bed sheets. With my bare hands, I also cleaned filthy catheters, soiled with excrement from sick patients, which were soaked in pots of chemicals. It was not fun. Today, catheters are disposable; not then.

While in college, I assisted the nurse at night with making sure the sick male patients took their medicine and helped remove and replace bandages for those who needed such interventions. I unloaded boxcars full of redwood, which was challenging because the backbreaking work left my hands full of splinters and breathing the dust inside the boxcars was unavoidable. I worked in a furniture-making factory doing all kinds of tasks, from assembly work, to cutting wood with huge electrical saws, to stacking freshly glued planks for different projects. I also worked in a glass company, unloading giant sheets of glass for the cutters and glazers. I waxed cars, did landscaping, mopped floors and scrubbed toilets in the men's dorm. One summer, I sold religious magazines with a team of students to help pay for my studies. However, most of our earnings went to pay for the transmission of the Volkswagen van that broke down during a trip from Chicago to St. Louis.

I worked hard and know how difficult it is to try to make ends meet with this type of work. Every one of those jobs put me closer to my goal of finishing school. That's why they were worth doing in spite of their difficulty. I have a profound respect for members of the workforce who must do all the time what I only had to do for a season.

Notwithstanding, I forgot to follow my own counsel once and paid the price for being disrespectful. It happened in Puerto Rico. I flagged a taxi cab to take me from the plush Plazas Las Americas mall to the Caribe Hilton Hotel near old San Juan. The cab looked tired and a bit worn out. Closing the door, I sat down and blurted out the first thing that crossed my mind: "This car has seen better days."

As soon as the words came out of my mouth, I sensed that I had crossed the line.

It was the driver's turn to talk.

"Listen, señor, don't you dare make insults about this car. This car has allowed me to put two of my children through college. My wife is next. She will be a school teacher in one more year."

Sensing his conviction and pride, I knew that I had bumped smack into a learning moment.

"Please forgive my insensitive comments... I was..."

"This is not a shabby car. This has been my most important bridge for changing the fortunes of my family. So, you need to be very careful about your comments, sir. I love this car. You are very lucky to be riding in it."

I got busted by a man who knew the real purpose and value of difficult work.

"This car has created wealth for our family!"

I congratulated him on his work ethic and for allowing me to ride in such an important vehicle. I meant it. He knew it. I gave him a big tip.

Education is costly, but worth it. Dr. Wayne Dyer put it best: "When you change the way you look at things. The things you look at change."

Since then, I have been driven in many limos and luxury vehicles, but never in such a meaningful one. I am glad he called me to task for my insensitive comments.

He allowed me to accept his discipline as an opportunity to recognize his dignity as a common worker with an uncommon vision for his family to excel through education.

STRATEGIES FOR SUCCESS

If today were the last day of my life, would I want to do what I am about to do today?" And whenever the answer has been "No" for too many days in a row, I know I need to change something.

Steve Jobs

a) **Persevere and always live by your words to excel.**

Remember Helen Keller!!! She was tempted to give up, but persevered: "Discouragement and weariness cast me down frequently; but the next moment the thought that I should soon be at home and show my loved ones what I had accomplished, spurred me on, and I eagerly looked forward to their pleasure in my achievement."

Follow her lead. When you look up to the people who love and invest in your achievements, you must get down to doing the hard work of succeeding in school and graduating several times over.

As you earn awards, excellent grades and recognitions in school, your loved ones get kudos and applause for their success in bringing you up with the right values.

John F. Kennedy was on point: "As we express our gratitude, we must never forget that the highest appreciation is not to utter words, but to live by them."

Talk and then "walk the talk" on the importance of education in your life. Sending home "I love you" emails, having conversations with your parents via cell phones, texting them messages and posting Facebook photos, as well as Skyping. These virtual face to face emotional visits may prove to be completely empty gestures.

Something else has to be going on, like providing those you love with updates and evidence of struggles and triumphs in your efforts to complete your program of study. No other gift will compare.

b) Excel to honor champions of equal opportunity in education.

If you are a member of a group that has experienced discrimination, please pay heed. Think of the heroic struggles of those who have worked at a great price to tear down walls of prejudice and inequality.

Because of their contribution, you and I have opportunities to study in order to improve our lives and work for a just society. Leverage your talents to improve our society as a prepared professional.

As a graduate, your new prestige and competencies will prove essential for keeping the doors of equal opportunity open. If you have benefited from their struggles, honor them through your academic success. The worst kind of ingratitude is for you to drop out of learning places today that did not allow members of your group to attend in the past. Find out everything that champions of civil rights and self-determination ever said about education and abide by their principles. If you love them, follow their counsel.

c) Graduate more than once; it's essential to your success.

Don't let your high school graduation be your last. There are people in your present journey and others in your future path who must serve as the inspiration for your continued climb to the head of the class. The more formal education you gain beyond high school, the better prepared you will be to improve the quality of your life and make our world and society a better place for all.

To work in the global economy, you will need more than a high school diploma. Not all jobs require a college degree. But, in the near future, that will change.

Even now, jobs with good incomes and benefits require more than a high school diploma. The jobs requiring a strong back and a willingness to work will continue to be exported to cheaper markets overseas. Jobs available close to home will not always pay a livable wage. To make ends meet, you might have to take two of those jobs.

You might want to read Nickel and Dimed: On (Not) Getting By in America by Barbara Ehrenreich. It will open your eyes to the harsh realities of working and not making ends meet. There is dignity in this type of work. Do it if you have to. Let it be a bridge that will take you from working with your hands and back to being able to work as an educated professional.

d) Share the bounties of your educational success with your elders.

There is a good chance some of you will see your

parents retire and collect small pensions and social security.

Because your parents will live a long time on a fixed income and likely have health issues, they might need help from you and their other children. They may not know it, but by investing in your education, they are also investing in their future. If you do not succeed today, they may suffer greatly tomorrow. When you excel and graduate, you are not just giving them a source of pride, but you may, through your economic success, allow them to have dignity and health as seniors.

For those of you who are first generation students who must excel in middle-class places of learning, what I am writing here must be taken to heart. Those parents without a lot of formal education will depend on you. My mother lived to thank me for disobeying her. After I got rejected by the military, she wanted me to go to the factory and work. By then, I was listening to my mentor and coach instead. I went to school.

Many years later, when she fell on hard times, I was able to take care of her. She lived to write a book and to have healthcare. My wife and I took care of her until her death. She was grateful that I chose to study before working. Love your parents enough to continue to study, even when they prefer that you go to work.

Study and excel first; they will live to thank you. Believe me, I know.

GETTING IT RIGHT CASE STUDY

Human progress is neither automatic nor inevitable... Every step toward the goal of justice requires sacrifice, suffering, and struggle; the tireless exertions and passionate concern of dedicated individuals.

Martin Luther King, Jr.

Melba Patillo Beals is one of my "sheroes." You must meet her. She is both amazing and inspiring! Melba and eight other African American youth volunteered to desegregate Central High School (CHS) in Little Rock, Arkansas in 1957. She had no idea just how dangerous or meaningful that mission would be.

Her decision to attend and the fierce opposition to integration by the white citizens of the city, the governor and racists from neighboring states put Melba and eight other high school teens (labeled the Little Rock Nine) on a collision course of historic proportions. Even the President of the United States got into the dispute, supporting Melba's and her friend's constitutional right to attend the all-white high school.

The Supreme Court had ruled on May 17, 1954 that racial segregation was inherently unequal. Three years later, Melba and her friends volunteered to be the first to attend the all-white school as the laws allowed. The governor, however, opposed such a move and sent members of the Arkansas National Guard to block their entry. He inflamed the passions of the white majority opposed to integration. Ugly mobs threatening violence gathered in front of CHS to stop the teens from going in. The Little Rock Nine arrived, but quickly had to flee for their lives. The story made national and international headlines.

President Eisenhower stepped into the fray, siding with the Little Rock Nine. He forced Governor Faubus to remove the National Guard troops from blocking the entrance to CHS and allow the students to enter the buildings (a governor of a state must enforce, not disobey federal laws). With US Army military escorts, Melba and her friends were reluctantly permitted entry into the school. Melba quickly found out that getting into CHS was the easy part. Once in the building, the nine students suffered racist driven violence, harassment and torturous persecution from the white students.

The awful truth is that a lot of whites preferred Melba and her friends dead rather than have their presence "pollute" their racially exclusive high school. The students, teachers and administrators, police, religious leaders, merchants and political leaders of the city and the state were all fiercely opposed to having black students attend CHS. However, Melba and her eight partners, with the support of the National Association for the Advancement of Colored People (NAACP), the courts, family members, and sheer will power to pursue justice through a quality education, would not be denied.

White parents taught their children attending CHS how to express hatred by inflicting physical pain and emotional injury on the black students. The plan was to hurt and intimidate the nine students into quitting. The teachers formed part of the conspiracy. When the assaults began, the police looked the other way. The few teachers and students who wanted to do the right thing were frustrated and prohibited from helping – or else. Nevertheless, a few took the risks and are celebrated by Melba in her book.

Read her book, Warriors Don't Cry, to walk with Melba through the halls of the high school from hell as she describes her daily struggles to stay alive and excel. She will become your "shero" as well. Melba was only 15 when the struggles to get a quality education began. Her losses were staggering.

She lost her innocence, naiveté and peace of mind. Her faith was put to the test, big time. The experience punched holes in her self-confidence. Salt was poured into her wounds. She suffered indignities that made shambles of her 16th birthday, cheapened her humanity and endangered her safety and that of her family.

The pain would not stop. It became so unbearable that she thought of killing herself. Here is a list of some of what she experienced:

- Chased by mobs shouting racial slurs

- Barely escaping the clutches of a rapist

- Harassing phone calls at all hours of the night

- Having her home under KKK surveillance 24/7

- Realizing that the police were part of the problem

- Dispersion of friends to different hostile classrooms

- Denial of participating in extra-curricular activities

- Suspension threats for acts of self-defense

- Taunts to invite aggression leading to expulsion

- Teachers refusing to help victims or to discipline culprits

- Helplessly watching friends get assaulted

- Stabbings with pencils and other sharp objects

- Tripping on the legs of bullies

- Dodging burning rolls of toilet paper while in stalls

- Being shoved down staircases

- Being befriended and later rejected by students to cause pain

- Being punched while walking through school hallways

- Wiping spit from face

- Finding her locker broken into and stuff missing

- Discovering peanut butter and broken glass on the seat of her chair

- Clothing damaged by ink, urine and smelly filth

- Being slapped in the face

- Gym showers suddenly turned to hot, scalding levels

- Clothes taken from gym shower area and put in toilets

- Deflecting exploding fire crackers tied to wires from her face

- Losing friends who did not want to be in harm's way

- Seeing her mom lose her job over school integration

- Black community anger over making waves

- Coping with the crisis of her parents' divorce

Melba confided in her beloved grandmother, India, about her desire to end it all through suicide. The two had a heart to heart talk on the outcome of such a decision. Snapping out of her desire to call it quits, Melba shares the meaning of her relationship to her family and how she became resilient and motivated to continue in her quest to excel:

"During those days I felt close to her, and I knew I had been silly for wanting to give up. Several times she looked at me and said, "Don't you know, child, how much I love you, how much your mama loves you?"

"Whenever you think about going away from this earth, think about how you'd break my heart and your brother's heart. You might as well take your mother with you because she'd be beside herself."… She made me get a project I really liked and encouraged me to keep on top of it. I chose the blast-off of the Explorer, the satellite that put our country into the space race… Grandma studied up on the topic, and we talked for hours while she taught me how to do the quilting for Mother's birthday present."

Melba returned to the tortuous conditions at CHS because she was loved by her family. Looking up to her loved ones meant getting down to the difficult work of excelling in school in spite of the adversity.

Melba wanted an education as much as, if not more than, a racist society did not want her to have it. She knew more education meant having more options. Getting out of oppressive circumstances required putting up with the painful reality impacting her and the other eight students. She put her life on the line to have access to what too many of us take for granted and do not always take seriously.

Education is the passport out of ignorance, out of poverty and out of hostile environments. It will also allow you to work where you live to dismantle walls of separation with educated people from every identity group in the community.

I have read her memoir, Warriors Don't Cry, twice and recommend that you read it at least once. In spite of their abuse and emotional turmoil, Melba and her peers finished that awful school year and advanced the cause of civil rights in our country. The Little Rock Nine are recognized as civil rights champions in the annals of history in the USA.

Go through the book and then let her book go through you. Feel the power of Melba being hated and refusing to hate in return. Apply her principles of resiliency and learn to bounce back from adversity. Adversity and not the easy life will build and shape your character. The ugly, horrible, abusive stuff that's causing injury today – if it does not destroy you, will make you stronger tomorrow. That's what happened to our "shero."

Keep your eyes on the prize. When you get knocked down, get up. Refuse to stay on the ground. The harder Melba got hit, the more determined her movements forward became.

Strip yourself from crippling excuses that frustrate your journey to the head of the class. Quit making a career of indulging in self-pity. Emulate Melba. She gave her family and those yearning for a more just society the gift of an educated self. Do likewise.

Live the truism: "Flee not from the storm; rather learn to dance in the rain."

Dare to thrive, achieve and excel in the face of dangerous distractions in hostile surroundings and against painful obstacles in your path. And may her force be with you!

CONCLUSION

Love yourself enough to want to excel and pay back the loan of education with the gift of an educated self. Then, honor your loved ones through your academic success. That means you must graduate several times over in your lifetime.

Reflect on your high school graduation and let that important rite of passage serve as a source of inspiration for future learning. The time in which we live requires that you prepare to work more with your head and less with your hands and back, the way our parents and great grandparents did.

It's important, as you transition from poverty to the professions, from blue collar work to white collar work, that you always respect the dignity of people who continue to be productive through manual labor. I didn't do that in San Juan and was busted by a taxi driver to mind my manners.

Lastly, remember the life and struggle of those who put their lives on the line to open up opportunities for the rest of us. Melba Patillo Beals is a case in point.

She, alongside the Little Rock Nine, suffered insults and indignities during a harsh and brutal time in our nation's history to pursue education. Her book, Warriors Don't Cry, is a source of inspiration for all generations who want to pay tribute to them by enrolling and graduating again and again so as to pay back the loan of education and make our world and society a more just and healthier place in which to live and work.

More Praise for Winning the Future

Samuel Betances distills a practical set of guiding principles and strategies for all teen and young adult learners, regardless of their race, culture or economic circumstances.

Dr. John R. Porter, Jr., Superintendent
Franklin- McKinley School District
San Jose, California

As a lifelong advocate for 'at-promise' students, I praise Dr. B's new book, where he reaches to the depths of his heart wrenching personal journey as a child to explain to us what it is to live in a life without hope. It is through his words that teach us once and for all how to truly serve the disadvantaged child in school and beyond. It is a 'read tonight' for every one whose passion it is to ensure no child is left behind.

Janet Grigg, Director
Justice Alma Wilson SeeWorth Academy
"We See the Worth of Every Child"
Oklahoma City, Oklahoma

What the author shares teaches the head, and touches the heart; as he instructs students, informs families and inspires educators at every level of instruction.

Carl R. Boyd, Advice Teacher
Mid-America Education Hall of Fame

This gem of a book is a refreshing change that will encourage you for a lifetime. There are many books whose advice you believe. This is a book whose advice you will follow. The wisdom from a life well lived in spite of adversity is a timeless gem that I thank this sage scholar for writing.

Dr. Rosita López, Professor
Northern Illinois University Leadership,
Educational Psychology & Foundation

This is a "must have" for all high school and college students! Betances turns personal roadblocks and frustrating experiences into an easy-to-follow guide of practical advice for teenagers—10 chapters, 10 steps. The book offers a concise description of proven tactics that have the power to change a student's life. I'm recommending this easy-to-read book to every high school student we serve.

Alfredo Calderón, Executive Director
Aspira Inc. of Pennsylvania

As a high school senior of the public school system, I found Dr. Betances' work truly motivating; his genuine voice and passionate language incite an inspirational spirit that adolescent readers can truly resonate with and utilize as a constant reminder of the triumph of the human spirit.

Karan Lall, High School Student and Author, <u>How to Score a 5: A Student's Guide to the AP Statistics Exam</u>, Caney Press

Winning the Future through Education- One Step at a Time is an important read. Whether you are a young person at risk seeking guidance, a person of comfort seeking a window on the challenges of a wider world, or a teacher or mentor of young people who wish to better understand the importance of their work and calling, this book of wisdom from a life well-lived will resonate with you. Dr. Samuel Betances is a sage.

Kyle Tong, *History Department Chair Columbus Academy*

Winning the Future is the perfect antidote for those who thought they had lost the past. Samuel Betances has given us more than a no-nonsense guide to common sense, he has given us strategies for success rather than excuses for failure. He has given educators and our young

people a resource book on how to move forward in life. The book is peppered with his personal stories of triumph rather than an account of tragedy. It is a remarkable contribution that should be read in schools from Guam to Puerto Rico and all those places in between.

Dr. Robert Underwood, President
University of Guam

Dr. B has an inspiring message for our youth—a simple, but challenging path to further their education and improve their chances for success in the future. He has the credibility to reach those most disadvantaged, because he has overcome nearly every possible obstacle to get to where he is today.

Jeffrey L Fowler Vice Admiral
U.S. Navy, (Ret)
Former Superintendent, U.S. Naval Academy

As I read this book, I imagined the outcomes of recreating Betances' model in our inner-city schools; if it was possible to replicate it 10 or 100 times over, our communities and cities would be transformed within one or two generations ... and with enough determination, this change would last forever.

Patricia Muñoz-Rocha, Principal
Instituto Health Sciences Career Academy
Chicago, Illinois

Inspiring. Motivating. Real. This book ignites that "fire in the belly" we all have, and provides a roadmap to success. It inspires you to conquer the world through education. I love this book! On behalf of my students and myself, thank you for writing this book, Dr. B! It will definitely be read by our high school students in our book club.

Amanda Ercilla Treviño, LCSW
HILT Institute Program Coordinator
Arlington, Virginia

BAM!! This is a must read for parents and students alike. Take it from a dean who has worked both in the US and now internationally, there has been no better "how to succeed in school" book written. I applaud the author for developing an easy to follow roadmap to success for all students. This is especially true for first generation college students.

Richard T. Johnson, Dean
International Programs
Texas A&M University/TEEX

This book serves as a call to action, providing students with clear and specific steps that will motivate them to succeed through reading and educational excellence.

Carlos Pérez, Chief Executive Officer
New Jersey Charter Schools Association

In this book, Dr. Betances incorporates an appropriate balance of theory and practice. His recommendations are directly aligned with many of the college readiness standards that have been identified in the Common Core State Standards. It's imperative that every student, educator, parent and policy maker to read this book and equally important, act on the steps to success which he describes explicitly throughout various chapters.

Dr. Sonya L. Whitaker, Superintendent
Fairmont School District 89, Lockport, IL

This book will inspire, rejuvenate, and encourage a continued quest for knowledge. Winning the Future through Education is a testament that you can be successful if given the tools, opportunity, and the innate belief and desire to accomplish a goal!

Dr. Joyce D. Kenner, Principal
Whitney M. Young High School, Chicago, IL

Not only is this book a treasure for students, it is a must have for parents and teachers!

Mary Christensen, M.Ed.,
Parent, Educator, Lifelong Learner
Pius XI High School, Milwaukee, WI

Informative without being preachy, Dr. Samuel Betances hits a rare note that will resonate with young people AND their parents. Using this book will help students avoid the pitfalls that slow academic acumen and chip away at self-esteem. As an educator who saw me in a couple of pages, I wish this were around when I was in school!

Ms. Gerlma A. S. Johnson, Principal
Amelia Earhart Elementary/Middle School,
Detroit, MI

This book serves as an excellent tool and roadmap for motivating students from low socio-economic backgrounds to excel.

Evelyn Rivera – Torres, Director Talent Search
University of Puerto Rico, Rio Piedras Campus

Few books focus on the experience of non-traditional students. Even less guide first-generation college goers. By anticipating future

*education, this book leads the pack in preparing
students to the challenges ahead.*

Dr. Abdín Noboa-Ríos, President
Innovative Consultants International, Inc.

*For the lifelong learner, this book reminds us that
without daily investment in ourselves, excellence
cannot be achieved.*

Mayor Michael B. Coleman
City of Columbus, OH

*In my generation we need something or someone
that will lend a helping hand and be "real" with
us. Throughout the book every step is clear and
understandable. Each step guides teens along the
path of success for good grades, graduating, and
engaging in life. I've taken one of the steps for my
own road of reaching achievement by completing
school tasks early. I was such a procrastinator.
Life for a teen is challenging, having a tool for
guidance is a privilege and this is exactly the job
this book attains. Also, it is a fun and easy read.*

Jadea Edmonds, Student
Booker T. Washington High School
Montgomery, AL

Exciting addition to the developmental education literature. It brings to life the struggle to "become" through an autobiographical account. It provides a blueprint for a student who is seeking to understand the process of self-actualization. It is an incisive statement of how one can rise through education from urban squalor to Harvard and beyond. Well done!!!

Jose M. Aybar, PhD
Claremont Graduate School

Samuel Betances shares his compelling personal narrative of moving from disillusionment with education to embracing the power of words, literally and figuratively, 'crossing a bridge called books.' Books lifted his spirit and increased his respect for the human condition. Reading sharpened his critical thinking and developed his coping skills. An influential mentor lifted Dr. Betances' goals and let him see that education was the key to his success and self-efficacy. Growing his word power in both English, and his native Spanish, deepened his comprehension and expanded his speaking vocabulary that Betances offers as just one step in attaining academic success.

Pamela A. Mason, Ed.D.,
Director of the Jeanne Chall Reading Lab
Harvard Graduate School of Education

About the Author

Samuel Betances is the author of **Ten Steps to the Head of the Class**. He is best known for keynoting and presenting workshops on educating and graduating students from poverty. With a compelling personal journey from dropping out of school to earning two graduate degrees from Harvard, he engages and challenges educators and students to excel.

Having worked at the US Department of Education and as a Professor of Sociology at Northeastern Illinois University in Chicago for 25 years, Dr. Betances is recognized for his advocacy of First Generation College Students. He has provided professional leadership and staff development training to over 1,112 public and private schools at home and abroad. Meaningful interactions with educators, students, parents and youth workers at high schools, colleges and universities have inspired him to write: **Winning the Future through Education**.

His children and grandchildren are products of the Chicago Public Schools. Samuel lives with his wife Laura in Chicago and Rio Grande, Puerto Rico.

Product Information

New Century Forum, Inc. is the publisher and a distributor of Dr. Samuel Betances' products.

Other books on education by the author include:

- Ten Steps to the Head of the Class: A Guide for Students

- Diez Pasos Hacia la Excelencia Estudiantil: Un Reto para los Estudiantes

Quantity Purchases

Companies, schools, professional groups, clubs and other organizations may qualify for special terms when ordering quantities of these products.

For more information or to order, contact:

New Century Forum, Inc.
5448 N. Kimball Ave.
Chicago, IL 60625
Phone: 773-463-1667

For more information about engaging Dr. Betances for keynotes, workshops, training and consulting, contact:

Souder, Betances and Associates, Inc.
Phone: 773-463-6374
Email: contactus@betances.com
Website: www.betances.com